The Accent of Success

A Practical Guide for International Students in U.S. Colleges

SECOND EDITION

Eric B. Shiraev and Gerald L. Boyd

Ann Arbor
University of Michigan Press

To John and Judy Ehle, Maria Grieg, Patricia Beckett, and Kay Haverkamp, who opened doors for us.

Acknowledgments

The authors would like to acknowledge the following people for their contributions to this book. In particular, we would like to thank Thomas Butler, John Ehle, Barbara Saperstone, Jeanne Morse, Bruce Mann, and Belle Wheelan for their relentless support of a multicultural educational environment and our professional efforts. For help in the development of this book, the authors would like to acknowledge Mary O'Neill and Kathy Lloyd, who have collaborated with us many times and have given us valuable advice on various topics. Many thanks go to our NVCC colleagues Florine Greenberg, Don Devers, Maurice L'Heureux, Elizabeth Tebow, Michelle Lewis, and Pam Stewart. We would also like to show appreciation to Mary Brooks (Eastern Washington University), Allison Rice (Hunter College), Dave Sperling (ESLcafe), Herbert Pierson (St. John's University), and Sergei Tsytsarev (Hofstra University) for their important contributions and insights. We gratefully acknowledge the helpful advice of David Levy (Pepperdine University), Fred Bemak and Rita Chung (George Mason University), and Cheryl Koopman (Stanford University). A special note of appreciation for their professionalism and personal courtesy is due to Michelle Williams and Sande Johnson at Prentice Hall, Gay Pauley at Holcomb Hathaway, and Sue Bierman.

For the **Second Edition**, we are indebted to Mary O'Neill for her excellent recommendations for revisions. We are also thankful for Lori Boyd's tireless editorial support. We thank Stephen Bennett for his comments and expertise related to F-1 visas. We would like to acknowledge our President, Dr. Robert Templin, and our Executive Vice President, Dr. John Dever, for their support for international students and their vision for our college's role in global learning. Finally, we thank Kelly Sippell at the University of Michigan Press for her patience, professionalism, and support.

Copyright © by the University of Michigan 2008
The first edition was published by Pearson Education, Inc., 2000
All rights reserved
Published in the United States of America
The University of Michigan Press
Manufactured in the United States of America

♾ Printed on acid-free paper

ISBN-13: 978-0-472-03256-3

2011   2010   2009   2008   4   3   2   1

Contents

Preface: **A Word for the Student**

This is a second edition of the book under the same title that was published a few years ago. Thanks to many great comments, encouragements, and suggestions from our readers, we have made some improvements and additions to this new edition. Most changes concern updates related to statistical materials. Although basic rules of admissions to U.S. universities and colleges remain the same as in 2001, there are other changes in the book: We give new examples and appeal to new facts. We use recent opinion polls and surveys. We have also included the results of our own research and interviews conducted over the past five years. Also, this edition has a fresh new look, which we hope the reader will appreciate.

* * *

In a way, we are all strangers. Very few of us stay in one place. We all came from somewhere. We move looking for knowledge, better lives, better opportunities, and new challenges. We search for peace, love, happiness, and freedom. We want to travel and explore. We try to find professions and occupations suited to our needs, skills, and talents. No matter what motivates you to study in the United States—a long-planned and awaited journey or a sudden opportunity—you are taking a decisive step in your life.

To be successful in college is not easy. It is especially tough if you are new to this country. The language, the customs, the rules, the weather—everything could become a new hurdle for you. There are many questions that can confuse any student: What is the correct visa? How do I choose the right college? What is the right program for me? How do I take notes in class? How do I get help? What shall I watch on television? How can I remain optimistic? This book addresses these and many other questions and problems that almost every international student will face on a college campus.

Our book will help you overcome the initial myths and fears related to visas and will help you understand higher education in the United States. It also advises how to plan your day and how to get the most from the printed and virtual sources around you. It discusses how to organize your semester, make appointments, and plan ahead. It gives tips on how and where to talk to your professor. It trains you in productive note-taking and essay writing. The book provides you with basic tools of critical thinking. It shows how to use

American television, newspapers, and the Internet more effectively for your education. It helps you understand customs in the United States. This book will teach you more about American conversations and greetings, celebrations and holidays, eating habits and shopping.

Once you make the decision to study in the United States, you will find that many advisors who have your best interest at heart will emerge. Listen to their advice, but make sure that you base your decisions on solid evidence. Let your decisions be informed by your own careful research. Once you have made a commitment to an institution, you should follow the process that the school presents to you and be timely in meeting your deadlines. Once you arrive in the United States, take advantage of the many resources available at your college or university.

We hope this book will steer you in the right directions. Remember that this will be a unique opportunity, so take responsibility for making it a productive and positive one. Good luck in your journey!

A Note for Students and Advisors

Obtaining visas related to education is a complicated process. People who are not qualified to give advice in this area often give students conflicting or confusing information. The Foreign Student Advisor at your school should be fully trained, and you should follow his or her advice.

The National Association of Foreign Student Advisors (NAFSA) provides information, training, and resources for Foreign Student Advisors. Much of what is presented in this book related to visas was either directly or indirectly influenced by the NAFSA Manual and the U.S. Department of State Code of Federal Regulations. Information about NAFSA can be found at *www.nafsa.org*.

Remember, however, that it is ultimately the U.S. Department of State that issues visas and the Department of Homeland Security that grants status and permits entry into the United States. It is their rules and regulations to which everyone must adhere.

PART 1

First Things

Y ou have made a very important life decision: You want to travel to the United States to study. Let us begin with the simple question: What are your educational goals? The answer, of course, will vary from individual to individual. Some people may want to come to the United States to study the English language. Some want to pursue a four-year degree at a university. Others want to earn the highest academic degree they can. Deciding upon your goal will help you to determine what you want to study and will help you select the best school in the geographic area of your choice. This is easier said than done. From the moment you decide to study in the United States until you attend the very first lecture, there will be many things to do. Applying to a school and getting the proper paperwork done is a very complicated process. But wait! Acceptance to a college or university is just the beginning of your journey. Once you arrive in America, you will realize that there are many, many issues, small and large, that you will need to address. For many, study abroad is like beginning a new life. Isn't that important enough to prepare for such an exciting journey?

CHAPTER 1

The United States Today: What Has and Has Not Changed since September 11, 2001

- With a population of more than 300 million, the United States is the third most densely inhabited country in the world and the third largest in terms of territory. Every year, the United States adds about 3 million new citizens. Almost 2.5 million of these are newborn babies, and about 500,000 people receive their U.S. citizenship by becoming naturalized citizens, which is a legal process. Today, compared to other nations, the United States remains the leading recipient of immigrants in the world.

- As a typical industrialized nation, the United States has a relatively low birth rate (an average woman gives birth to two children), but at the same time it has one of the highest life expectancy rates in the world: This generation is expected to live approximately 78–80 years. Currently, more than 20 percent of the population in this country is younger than 14, and about 15 percent of Americans are age 65 or older.

- The United States has the largest and most technologically dominant economy in the world. One of the most universal numbers measuring the strength of a nation is the "per capita GDP" or average amount of goods and services produced for one person. In the United States this figure is $44,000 compared with China's GDP of $8,000 or India's GDP of about $4,000.

- Seventy-eight percent of the people living in the United States work in service areas including education, local and federal government, health care, and retail and food service. Less than 1 percent of Americans work in the agriculture sector, and 21 percent work in manufacturing.

- The vast majority of American families have at least one car. Almost 70 percent of American adults own a home, according to a 2006 study by the Center for American Progress.

After September 11, 2001

When Americans say "nine eleven," everyone knows it means September 11, 2001. On that fateful day, four groups of terrorists boarded civilian airplanes and attacked the two buildings of World Trade Center in New York City and the Pentagon building near Washington, DC. The fourth plane crashed in Pennsylvania. More than 3,000 people were killed on that day. Have America and its people changed because of September 11th?

Ask this question of Americans who lived in this country before "nine eleven," and you will receive, of course, different answers. Many people will say that, indeed, the country has changed considerably. For example, many Americans express serious concerns about the safety of their country and their own families today. The terrorist attacks were a very emotional event for all Americans. We, the authors of the book, live near Washington, DC, and were working just a few miles away from the site of the Pentagon crash. Almost all of the people we spoke to during the days following September 11—our friends and neighbors, students, professors, even people on the street—expressed anxiety and serious concerns about their future. In the fall of 2001, many Americans were afraid to fly and preferred to drive a car or take a train to visit relatives or friends in other parts of the country. All airlines operating in the United States reported a substantial decrease in tickets purchased by Americans at the end of 2001. Some people even decided to leave big cities and move to small towns, feeling that life would be safer there. Overall, observers noticed that many Americans began to pay serious attention to their country's security.

After the initial period of uncertainty and anxiety in 2001, life eventually went back to a level of normalcy. Some people actually say that their lives haven't been affected much by the terrorist attacks. Today, life goes on much as it did 10 or 20 years ago. Every morning, as usual, children go to school. Working adults drive or take mass transit to their offices and shops, and others remain very busy at home taking care of household chores. For most, however, there is a lingering sense of caution and vulnerability, and many families have been permanently devastated by the horrible attacks.

Americans were not the only ones affected by the events of 9/11; there were casualties from many other countries, and a great outpouring of concern worldwide. Many people changed their plans to visit the United States, fearing for their safety, and there was a severe and immediate drop in the number of international students entering the country. The United States government reacted immediately to protect its borders and made significant changes in its structure, policies, and procedures related to immigration, visas, and international travel. Regulations and procedures were tightened and remain focused on maintaining the appropriate level of security for the country.

Since 2002, college enrollment has increased in all states. Americans celebrate national and religious holidays, eat out with their families in restaurants, travel to various places, and visit foreign countries. More Americans fly on passenger airplanes today than ever before in history. A 2005 report issued by the U.S. Department of Transportation indicated that, by 2004, the number of passengers traveling using commercial airlines had exceeded pre–September 11 numbers and has continued to rise (U.S. Department of Transportation 2005).

In general, people's perceptions of their lives are based on many factors and circumstances. To some individuals, their lives have changed for the worse, while to others their situation today is much better than yesterday. Yet there are certain general changes that are possible to see or measure. What specific changes took place in the United States after the events of September 11, 2001?

Immigration and Travel Procedures

The rules to enter the United States and other travel procedures for internationals arriving to America have become more complicated. Almost everyone who lives in a different country and has traveled to the United States before and after 2001 can say that the application process and opportunities to obtain a visa have become, in general, more difficult and timely. The U.S. government has given instructions to all consular sections of the U.S. embassies abroad to make changes in the procedures to obtain a visa. These changes are not intended to keep international guests and students away from the United States. Rather, the most important goal of the changes is to make sure that everyone who enters the United States has good intentions and doesn't want to harm Americans or their interests. Unfortunately, in many instances it seems that the changes are resulting in delays. Overall, many people wait for a long time to get a business, student, or tourist visa to visit the United States. Obviously, such delays and restrictions do not make people happy, and many feel that such restrictions are inefficient and wrong. It is our hope that these limiting measures are only temporary.

Today, everyone entering the United States must be fingerprinted and photographed by the inspection officers. The U.S. government also requires airlines to provide the lists of passengers in advance of all international flights to America. This allows the government to check the list of passengers against the Terrorist Screening Database (TSDB) to identify people who may be considered "unwelcome" in the United States. Such individuals are typically political activists belonging to various organizations suspected of terrorism or helping terrorist groups. Therefore, an ordinary individual who has never been connected with violent groups or organizations has very little chance to be singled out by this procedure.

To reduce delays, most American airports have made significant changes to improve service and expedite the admission of international guests. For example, the international terminal at Dulles Airport near Washington, DC, has been renovated significantly to accommodate international passengers. It is easy to notice that the line of international guests is frequently moving as fast as the line of American citizens going through passport control checkpoints.

Specific visa and immigration requirements are discussed in Chapter 2.

Attitudes about International Visitors

Overall, international business travel and tourism to the United States decreased in 2001–2003. This negative trend did not last long, however. According to official reports by the U.S. Department of Commerce, international tourists have brought more than $105 billion to the U.S. economy since 2005. There are more than 50 million international visitors every year, and their number keeps growing! Occasionally, some inaccurate rumors or some media reports suggest that Americans, since 2001, have become intolerant and even rude toward international visitors and immigrants. This is not true! In reality, the vast majority of Americans maintain a tolerant, friendly, and welcoming attitude toward guests from foreign countries. Public opinion studies confirm this observation. Seventy to eighty percent of Americans answering survey questions in 2003–2007 said that they have either positive or very positive views of international tourists and guests. According to national opinion polls, the vast majority of Americans don't want to limit tourism and student exchanges.

There are many reasons why American people accept and appreciate international guests. We will mention just two of them. First, there is what some people would say is a traditional cultural attitude where Americans respect international guests. America calls itself, "the nation of immigrants." Unlike most countries in the world, the majority of the people and their ancestors came from other parts of the world. Each year, more than half a million individuals become U.S. citizens. In addition, the United States annually admits from 50,000–70,000 refugees who are fleeing their home countries because of religious or ethnic oppression and violence.

The other reason for welcoming attitudes is economic. For example, the hotel, restaurant, tourism, and entertainment industries certainly need as many international guests as possible. The more people they accommodate and feed, the more money they make. Between May and September, restaurants and hotels in big cities rely significantly on international tourists.

Nevertheless, many Americans express serious concerns about illegal immigration. Determining who has the right to come, work, and stay in the United States is difficult. One 2006 poll (Shiraev and Sobel 2006) found that Americans were almost evenly split on illegal immigration issues. One-half of American people wanted to give everyone a "temporary" working status, while others rejected this option, saying that every person should come to this country legally. Other opinion polls show that people want to keep their country's borders protected. For example, a 2006 FOX News poll found that 91 percent of Americans believe that their country has the right to restrict immigration, and only 7 percent believe that the country should keep open borders (Shiraev and Sobel 2006). A majority of Americans believe that the rules according to which people can get a visa to enter the United States should become more restrictive.

In sum, the American people welcome guests from over the world but prefer to make sure that law and order prevail.

Changes at School

Ask students or professors in any university or college in the United States, and almost everyone will say that international students are more than welcome to come and study in this country. International students are eagerly anticipated and treated with kindness and respect. In fact, the attitudes at university campuses in America clearly reflect the overall atmosphere of the nation. Most international guests who come to the United States to study, learn, or do business are very welcome. In fact, according to the 2007 Open Doors report, 582,984 international students study in the United States. These students contribute $14.5 billion to the U.S. economy (Institute of International Education 2007).

Nevertheless, some important changes took place in colleges and universities after September 11, 2001. Today, for example, school administrators pay attention to international students who register for classes but do not show up. We certainly understand that there are many reasons why a student pays tuition but doesn't attend lectures. A person can be sick or very busy trying to resolve a family problem or another emergency situation. Some students may leave the country for important personal reasons (such as illness in the family, wedding, etc.), and they don't inform the authorities about the absence. In these cases, a problem may occur because school administration now has to make sure that the person who was supposed to study is, in fact, studying. We offer more detail on this in Chapter 2.

This may appear to some students as unnecessary or excessive attention to students' personal lives. On the other hand, we all must realize that although we have the right to do what we consider important, universities and colleges also have the right to verify who attends classes and who does not. It is very easy to avoid complications and potential problems if the student simply informs his or her professor, department chair, counselor, or a dean about the temporary absence and the reasons for not being in class. According to a 2006 Public Agenda Foundation poll (Shiraev and Sobel 2006), tighter control over international students who come to our colleges and universities to study was supported by almost 80 percent of Americans. This topic and the issue of attendance will be discussed several times in this book.

It is a mistake to think that, except for a few restrictions, nothing else has changed in the universities and colleges. There are, in fact, many welcoming changes that have taken place in many other areas of college life over the past several years. For example, significant changes have taken place in several academic programs, especially in the fields of history, social science, and political science. You will find out very soon how much attention colleges and universities pay to the disciplines related to foreign countries and cultures, international relations, world languages, comparative studies, international business, and international law! These subjects have been important and popular in the past; today, their popularity has significantly increased. There are more classes offered related to international and global issues, more discussion of world events is supported, and more international events take place on campus.

Looking for Answers

Following the events of 2001, many Americans began to ask why these terrorist acts were committed against their country. In fact, this was the first attack ever in the United States since 1814 when the British troops occupied portions of American territory and captured Washington, DC, the United States capitol. This most recent tragic event made most Americans think about their country and its role in international affairs.

The United States is a country founded on the ideas of fundamental political freedoms where people are accustomed to expressing their free opinions about any issue. Unlike many other countries in the world, Americans may speak and write without restraint about the government, the President, the Congress, and the country in general. At different times, many people may criticize the government and the President, but support them at other times. Not every American shares the same opinion about why or who was responsible for the events of September 11th. Americans also disagree on whether or not the American government was right or wrong to start the recent wars in Afghanistan and Iraq.

In trying to find answers, many Americans express critical views about their own government and its foreign policies. This is not something unique about the American people. Sociologists and political scientists will certainly show that over the last 60 years, Americans have been in general disagreement with each other about the country's foreign policy (Shiraev and Sobel 2006). Some people support the policies of the government, suggesting that America has the right to protect and guarantee stability and peace in the world. Others have different opinions, suggesting that the United States has no business telling other countries how to live their lives. And still others say that regardless of the U.S. foreign policy, there will be many people around the world who simply dislike America and the values for which it stands, reasoning that no matter what kind of foreign policy the United States has, there will always be criticism against it. Yet some say that the United States must engage in international affairs but handle it differently by sharing and helping other countries rather than using its military power. Many people today believe that a collective action through international organizations is better than doing things alone. For instance, more than 61 percent of Americans maintain a mostly or very favorable opinion of the United Nations (Shiraev and Sobel 2006). According to several national surveys, a majority of Americans take considerable pride in a few features of U.S. foreign policy. Most remarkably, they take great satisfaction in "helping other countries when natural disasters strike": An impressive 83 percent of respondents give the government high marks (Shiraev and Sobel 2006).

Overall, many important changes took place in the lives of American people: Americans today read more about international relations and other countries. The average American wants to know more about the events in the world. People continue to travel to foreign countries to learn and compare. According to a 2006 study by Harvard University and the *Washington Post* (Shiraev and Sobel 2006), 55 percent of Americans have either visited or lived in a foreign country and the number of people traveling abroad keeps rising.

Americans' Opinions

Despite the changes that are taking place in the world today and despite tensions and discussions about the United States past and future, Americans as people, on the whole, represent a happy nation. The Pew Research Center, a leading international public opinion center, conducted a survey in 2007 (Shiraev and Sobel 2006) that asked this simple question: "*How would you say things are these days in your life—are you happy?*" More than 85 percent of people said that they were very happy or somewhat happy. Despite some critical comments you hear from your American friends regarding high gasoline prices, traffic problems, and environmental issues, America, in general, is a nation of optimistic people. For example, 52 percent of Americans, according to a 2006 Economic Policy Institute Survey, believe that the quality of their lives is better now than that of the previous generations (Shiraev and Sobel 2006). Only 11 percent, which is little more than one in ten people, believes that the quality of life is worse. About one-third of people believe that the quality has not changed much over the years. This means that one out of two U.S. citizens believes that she or he lives better than his or her parents 20 or 30 years ago (Shiraev and Sobel 2006).

American people maintain diverse opinions on a variety of issues. On one hand, this is a nation of people who believe in science and technology. Americans are exposed to information on a daily basis; 99 percent of Americans watch at least some television every day. More than 230 million people in this country use the Internet and email for their communications. More than 30 percent of Americans have received college degrees (Greenberg Research 2006).

Americans are a pragmatic nation. They believe in reason and common sense. Yet America is also a religious nation. About 95 percent of Americans say they believe in God. This number hasn't changed since the 1950s. Another opinion poll (*Time*/SRBI 2006) conducted in 2006 showed that 80 percent of people in the United States believe in miracles. Most Americans express environmental concerns and believe that the government and private businesses should do more to reduce pollution. On the other hand, according to a 2007 study by the Associated Press and America Online, 66 percent of all American families own big vehicles such as a mini-van, pick-up truck, or SUV.

In the media, we often hear about how easy it is to obtain a divorce in America and that many people do not give serious attention to marriage. Opinion polls show that more than 75 percent of Americans believe that if a marriage does not go well, the couple has the right to seek divorce. However, statistics show that more than 70 percent of married Americans have never been divorced, and only 20 percent—one couple out of five—have been divorced once (7 percent divorced twice).

These are just a few examples of diversity in actions and opinions. People in the United States represent a very large and diverse nation. Learn to understand American life from different perspectives. Talk to people, ask them to express their opinion, and try to understand their position. The more questions you ask, the more complete picture of the American life you will obtain.

End Note

This is the only section in *The Accent of Success, Second Edition,* that addresses the tragic events of 9/11. The rest of the text has been updated to reflect some changes in practice and statistics. The book remains a guide for studying in the United States, which we consider to be a wonderful and valuable opportunity.

CHAPTER 2

Colleges in the United States

The following scenario is very familiar to us and exemplifies the misconception that people have about coming to the United States to study. The myth is that you can quickly run through a "grocery list" of things to do and then hop on a plane and come to the United States. It is much more complicated than that, and those who take short cuts end up paying extra for their haste in time and money.

My home telephone rang late in the evening. It was a long-distance caller, a son of my good old friend, dialing from the other side of the planet to apologize for such a late intrusion and to tell me that he had finally made a decision to study in United States.

"Have you already applied for a particular school?" I asked.

"No," he replied.

"Did you choose a school?"

"No."

"Do you want to apply for an ESL program first?"

"I don't know."

"Do you know how much will it cost?"

"Not exactly."

"Do you realize that it is too late to apply for the fall?"

"No. I thought in America you don't have to wait or do this paperwork."

"Listen," I finally told him, "I will send you an email about what to do and how to apply for school in the United States. However, be prepared to become a student in a year and a half, not earlier."

"I am sorry," he interrupted me. "May I arrive on a tourist visa and then get into college? It will be easier for me."

Now it was my turn to say, "No, that would not be a good idea."

Selecting a School

A great deal of planning needs to be done before making the decision to study here. The United States is a country with more than 4,000 colleges and universities, so one of the first steps involved in preparation is to decide which school you would like to attend. You may have a particular city or region in mind where you would like to study or a specific educational program in which you are interested. Your decisions should be made thoughtfully and carefully. Many people have wasted valuable time and money by selecting the wrong institution for their educational goals. It is important to do some productive research for yourself. Many college guides are available in book form and on the Internet that provide detailed descriptions about colleges, and some even rate the schools. Some popular titles are listed in the Appendix (page 186).

Check the libraries in your community and local colleges or universities to see if they have college guides available. If they cannot be obtained locally, or if they are outdated, then buy them. Most of these titles retail for under $30 and are well worth the investment. Buy at least one.

Numerous websites serve as sources for college reviews. For example, most search engines like Google™ and Yahoo® have links to review sites, or they can connect you to a list of sites. In addition, most institutions have their own websites. When you are looking up colleges on the Internet, keep in mind that websites serve not only as sources of information but also as marketing tools. Therefore, you should talk to as many people as you can to get a balanced profile of a particular school. Sometimes a personal reference can be more valuable and accurate than the printed materials sent out by the school. However, be careful not to allow one good or bad experience from another student to determine your overall opinion. Always try to get at least a second, third, or fourth judgment before making a decision.

Types of Post-Secondary Schools

It is often said that there is a college or university for everyone in the United States, and this is very close to being true. Of the more than 4,000 colleges and universities in the United States, you'll find a range from very large research universities to very small liberal arts colleges. In addition, there are colleges that only offer the first two years of an undergraduate degree or mainly coursework that supports occupations. Any one of these might be suited for a given student, depending on his or her personal goals. There is no standard model that all colleges or universities follow; however, there are some general categories based on the kinds of degrees students can earn. It is extremely important when selecting a school that you find one that offers the program and degree that will satisfy your educational plans. For instance, you would not want to apply to a two-year community college if you already have your bachelor's degree in your own country. You would want to select a university that has a graduate program in your field of study.

One of the unique aspects of education in the United States is that there is very little direct regulation by the federal (national) government. Education for the most part has been left to state and local governments and private enterprises. Most institutions are initially identified as public or private based on the way in which they are primarily funded for operation.

There are many ways to get information about the quality of a college or university. Most colleges go through a process of accreditation to demonstrate that they meet a standard of "excellence" (see page 20). Also, many publications rank colleges and universities based on certain criteria deemed important. The magazine *U.S. News & World Report* ranks institutions of higher education annually, and many institutions feel that this is an important measure. It is extremely important for you to do some research to establish where it is that you want to study and to fully understand the quality and reputation of that institution in relationship to other colleges and universities in the United States. Not everyone can go to the prestigious Ivy League or other elite schools, but there are many choices outside the premiere institutions that routinely deliver an excellent education.

Public Colleges and Universities

Public colleges and universities receive a significant amount of their operating budgets from the state governments in which they reside, and they must follow the same guidelines as other state-funded, government agencies in their states. In other words, public institutions must serve the needs of all of the taxpayers of the state, making them somewhat limited in how specialized they can be. For example, a public institution could not identify itself as representing a particular religious denomination. This, however, would be perfectly fine for a private institution.

The funds allocated (given) by a state to a particular college or university are used to offset the cost of tuition for residents of that particular state. At public institutions you will find an "in-state" tuition rate for residents and an "out-of-state" tuition rate for non-residents. Most international students who intend to study in the United States on a student or exchange visa will have to pay out-of-state tuition rates that can be much higher than in-state rates. For example, the undergraduate tuition rates for full-time study at an average-size public university per academic year (nine months that include fall and spring semesters) could be $5,000 for in-state tuition and as much as $18,000 for out-of-state tuition. There are a few exceptions to this general trend, but there are visas—for instance, diplomatic visas—that allow students to get in-state rates after residency requirements have been met.

Private Colleges and Universities

Private colleges and universities do not receive a large part of their operating budgets from the state. Their funding comes primarily from tuition, alumni (former students) donations, and religious and other private sources. Private colleges generally have the same tuition rates for all students, which can range from $15,000 to $35,000 per year and higher. Many of the most elite or prestigious colleges and universities in the United States are private institutions, and they do not fall under the same regulatory restrictions that public schools must follow. Because of this, private institutions have the ability to serve more narrow or specialized student categories if they so choose. For example, many colleges and universities are primarily supported by religious denominations. Also, some private institutions are exclusively for women. Not all private colleges and universities are specialized; some are independent from any particular organization and have a great deal of diversity in their student population.

Whether an institution is public or private may not make much difference to an international student. These institutions also range in size from 600 to 33,000 or more students, and this may be a more important factor. How well would you fit in to a small liberal arts college that focuses primarily on a well-rounded undergraduate experience? Are they prepared to handle the special needs of international students? At a school that has 33,000 students, how much individual support can you expect to get? These are important questions, and often a good recommendation from an international student who has studied or is studying at the institution can be of help.

Statements of Purpose/Mission Statements

You should be very clear about a school's goals and mission before selecting it. One way to find out the affiliation of a school is to look in the school's catalogue or website for their mission statement or statement of purpose. Please consider the following examples (these descriptions were taken from each school's webpages). Baylor University, a well-known and respected university in Texas that is affiliated with the Baptist Church, has a very clear mission statement:

> The mission of Baylor University is to educate men and women for world-wide leadership and service by integrating academic excellence and Christian commitment within a caring community.

The University of Notre Dame, a highly respected school in Indiana, is affiliated with the Catholic Church. It describes itself as:

> . . . a Catholic academic community of higher learning, animated from its origins by the Congregation of Holy Cross.

Brigham Young University, an esteemed university in Utah that is affiliated with the Mormon Church, has as its mission statement:

> The mission of Brigham Young University—founded, supported, and guided by the Church of Jesus Christ of Latter-Day Saints—is to assist individuals in their quest for perfection and eternal life. That assistance should provide a period of intensive learning in a stimulating setting where a commitment to excellence is expected and the full realization of human potential is pursued.

Smith College, a prestigious women's college in Massachusetts, has the following statement of purpose:

> Since its founding in 1871, Smith College has provided women of high ability and promise an education of uncompromising quality. A world-class faculty of scholars are fully engaged with their students' intellectual development, and an open curriculum encourages each student to explore many fields of knowledge. Mentors for scholarship, leadership and service, across all spectrums of endeavor, allow Smith students to observe different models of achievement, then set their own course with conviction.

In contrast, the mission of the University of Maryland, a large public research university states:

> The University of Maryland, College Park, is a public research university, the flagship campus of the University System of Maryland, and the original 1862 land-grant institution in Maryland. It is one of only 61 members of the Association of American Universities (AAU). In keeping with the legislative mandates of 1988 and 1999, the University of Maryland is

committed to achieving excellence as the State's primary center of research and graduate education and the institution of choice for undergraduate students of exceptional ability and promise. While the University has already attained national distinction, it intends to rank among the very best public research universities in the United States. To realize its aspirations and fulfill its mandates, the University advances knowledge, provides outstanding and innovative instruction, and nourishes a climate of intellectual growth in a broad range of academic disciplines and interdisciplinary fields. It also creates and applies knowledge for the benefit of the economy and culture of the State, the region, the nation and beyond.

K–12, Undergraduate, and Graduate Education

In the United States, education is required by law, and children must generally go through 12 years of study from first through twelfth grades. These twelve levels of study are generally broken up into Elementary School, which is first through fifth grades, Middle School, which is typically sixth to eighth grades, and Secondary School (High School), which is typically ninth through twelfth grades. A preparatory level called kindergarten or pre-school falls before first grade. There are variations of how the grades are distributed, and there are special programs that combine secondary and college-level work. The public school system is often referred to as the K–12 system, which means the kindergarten through twelfth grade system.

Students who graduate from secondary school are prepared to enter the workforce, get specific job training, go to college, or do all of these together. Students who are not able to graduate from secondary school have the option to work and/or get job training. To qualify for admission into a college or university, these students must complete an adult or alternative high school program, or pass the General Education Diploma (GED) test. The GED can serve as an alternative to a high school diploma. There are exceptions to this rule; many community colleges, for example, have an "open door" admission policy that allows anyone over the ages of 18 or 19 to take classes. However, students without a high school diploma or a GED may be limited to non-degree study and will always be at a disadvantage should they decide on further study beyond the community college.

Undergraduate education generally refers to the first four years of study at a college or university that leads to a degree. The two most common undergraduate degrees are the two-year associate's degree given by most junior colleges and community colleges, and the four-year bachelor's degree given by colleges and universities. These degrees are divided into different areas based on the nature of their curricula (set of courses). The most common areas are Science (A.S. or B.S.), Arts and Letters (A.A. or B.A.), Fine Arts (B.F.A.), and Education (B.Ed.). Note that these are general categories that can vary among colleges.

The bachelor's degree is normally awarded after completing 120 semester credit hours of generally specified coursework. The bachelor's degree has a required number of core or general education courses and then upper-level courses in a major area of study. Students officially identify their program of study by referring to it as their major. Schools divide their programs and departments based on these majors. For example, a student who plans on going into business might major in business, marketing, or accounting. A student interested in computers might major in computer science or information systems. Students interested in politics might major in public affairs, international relations, or political science. Carefully read the college catalog from the schools in which you are interested to make sure they have a major that covers your area of interest. You will be asked to indicate your intended major on your application. This information will be necessary for the paperwork needed to secure an entry visa. There is often a great variety of individual choice in selecting a major, and you have the option to change majors. Be careful though: Students who change majors too often waste valuable time and are sometimes unable to graduate in four years. Colleges and universities in the United States have academic counselors and advisors available to work individually with students on their academic plans. You may or may not be familiar with the role and function of academic counseling, but you should take full advantage of this service.

> ### ⭐ A Useful Tip
>
> The first year of study is called the freshman year, the second is the sophomore year, the third is the junior year, and the fourth is the senior year. Students are officially referred to as freshmen, sophomores, juniors, and seniors, based on the number of credits they have completed.

Academic counselors are at the institution for the sole purpose of helping students to plan and to understand the complicated process of completing a degree. You should become familiar with this office before registering for your first class and visit the office regularly until you graduate. Understand that there is a difference between personal counseling (which focuses on the issues of the individual self) and academic counseling (which focuses on an individual's progress toward the educational goals set). Most colleges and universities have offices for both functions, but all accredited institutions have at least one office that is responsible for academic counseling.

After completing an undergraduate program, many people enter the workforce if their undergraduate degree satisfies their needs. However, some people continue studying in graduate or professional programs after completing their bachelor's degree. Several bachelor's degree programs serve as preparation for a professional program—for example, law school or medical school. Also, some bachelor's degree programs do not give enough instruction in a specific area to prepare a student to work productively in that field, so more focused study is given at the graduate level. Because of tough competition in the job market, a graduate degree can often influence a hiring or promotion decision.

There are many kinds of graduate degrees. For example, the master's degree is generally 30 to 36 semester credits of focused study beyond the bachelor's degree and usually requires a final thesis (research) paper. The doctorate level is generally 60 to 65 credits beyond the master's degree and requires a dissertation (research) paper that represents an original contribution to the field of study. Professional degrees are the Juris Doctorate (J.D.) for lawyers and the Doctor of Medicine (M.D.) degree. These two degrees involve three to five years of study beyond the bachelor's degree.

The Academic Calendar

No specific calendar is required by law for colleges or universities in the United States. For the most part, colleges and universities follow the same general calendar, with slight variations. The majority of institutions of higher education follow a semester system, although there are a few, particularly community or technical schools, that follow a quarter system. The quarter system divides the year into four quarters that generally cover ten weeks each.

A semester system generally consists of two main semesters of 16 weeks called fall and spring semesters, with an optional summer term that often ranges from 8 to 12 weeks. The fall term is generally when new students are admitted to the institution; it usually begins at the end of August or early September and runs until mid-December. The spring term generally runs from mid-to-late January through May. The summer term often runs from early June to mid-August. International students studying on F-1 or J-1 visas are generally required to be full-time students during the fall and spring terms. Summers may be optional, depending on when you are entering the institution. Make sure that you are fully aware of your enrollment responsibilities. This must come directly from your Foreign Student Advisor.

Accredited or Non-Accredited Schools

No government agency directly oversees the quality of post-secondary education in the United States. This is one reason why you must be certain that the school you select is a credible institution. It should meet or exceed a minimum set of standards and be confirmed through a voluntary process of accreditation by a regional or national accrediting body. Accreditation is confirmation that a thorough external review of an institution has been done and that the institution meets a set of agreed upon standards in its operations. Regional accreditation covers all aspects of a college or university. The prevailing professional association of a field generally does national accreditation, and it generally accredits programs within a university.

There are six regional accrediting bodies: the Southern Association of Colleges and Schools, the New England Association of Schools and Colleges, the Middle States Association of Colleges and Secondary Schools, the North Central Association of Colleges and Secondary Schools, the Northwest Association of Schools and Colleges, and the Western Association of Schools and Colleges. These regional accrediting bodies are registered with the U.S. Department of Education, and all accredit both public and private institutions.

Other national accreditation bodies accredit professional programs. For example, the American Bar Association (ABA) accredits law schools. All states have regulations that require graduation from an accredited law school in order to receive a license to practice law in that particular state. This type of regulation extends to many fields, particularly those that involve the well-being of individuals. Medical schools and dental schools are other examples.

Liberal Arts, Research, and Land Grant Schools

Many colleges and universities have a historical character that they try to maintain. This is often reflected in their curriculum (set of courses) and in their missions. In the way that major corporations and large companies develop identities that define who they are, many colleges and universities have characteristics that make them unique. For most institutions, it is important that they preserve, develop, and market that character over time. For example, at the second oldest college in the United States, the College of William and Mary, colonial roots have been maintained although it is clearly a state-of-the-art college; a visitor on campus today can feel the history of the buildings and grounds. The Massachusetts Institute of Technology, which has a heavy research mission in the areas of science and technology, exhibits an unmistakably innovative character reflected through its architecture and grounds. Some schools identify themselves as *liberal arts* institutions or as having a liberal tradition. What they mean is that their curriculum will be very focused in the humanities. The purpose of these institutions is to cultivate minds and to create well-rounded citizens who can contribute to the culture and preserve traditional democratic values. *Research* universities are heavy in the math, science, and technical areas, and they stress the importance of developing the knowledge base. A research university will have departments that are found in liberal arts institutions, but the major resources generally go to the math, science, and engineering areas.

In your search for a school, you may run into the term *land grant institution.* Land grant colleges and universities have their own unique beginning. They were initially founded on the basis of two initiatives from the federal government, one in 1862 and one in 1890, where the U.S. government gave each state a piece of land to be used to start colleges and universities. These institutions were formed to serve the rural population and special populations not being well served by existing schools. Most of these schools had an agricultural and technical curriculum. Many land grant institutions have broader course offerings now but remain strong in the research tradition.

Post-Secondary Institutions: Basic Distinctions*

Junior Colleges

Junior colleges offer general education courses that lead to an associate's degree (two-year) in the arts (A.A.) or sciences (A.S.). These are either public or private institutions that usually serve to move students through transfer into a bachelor's degree program at a college or university. They normally have agreements with other colleges or universities that make admission easier for junior college graduates. Even though the faculty may be required to conduct research, teaching is the primary function of junior colleges. Some of them have on-campus housing, but most do not.

---

*Based on Carnegie Classification of Institutions of Higher Educations, Carnegie Commission on Higher Education.

Vocational/Technical Institutes

Training is the main function of these institutions. They offer a variety of programs in specific skill areas that prepare students specifically for employment. The programs vary in length but are generally less than two years. Vocational/technical schools can be public or private, and many are proprietary (they make a profit like a business). Some, particularly the public institutes, offer associate degrees; however, most primarily offer certificates that enable students to show their qualifications to enter a trade. Cosmetology, real estate, heating and air conditioning repair, and automotive repair are areas that commonly have certificate programs that lead to licensure for employment. The programs are generally in occupational and technical areas not served by other post-secondary institutions or professional schools, such as training in electronics, cosmetology (hairstyling and makeup), English as a Second Language (ESL), truck driving, office skills, computers, and culinary arts (cooking and baking). The list of these kinds of schools is much longer than we have provided here. These institutes normally do not have on-campus housing.

Comprehensive Community Colleges

These primarily public institutions offer courses that lead to an associate's degree (a two-year degree), general education for transfer to a college or university, and vocational/technical coursework. Community colleges generally have agreements with other colleges and universities that make transferring easier. Teaching and training, not research, are the primary focuses of these institutions. Community colleges normally do not have on-campus housing.

Four-Year Colleges

These colleges offer coursework leading to a bachelor's degree in the arts (B.A.) or sciences (B.S.), which normally takes four years of full-time study. A four-year college may offer a two-year associate's degree (A.S., A.A.) in a few subject areas, but they emphasize the bachelor's degree. Teaching is the primary function of these institutions, though the faculty may be required to have their own research agendas that along with teaching are part of their job requirements. Many four-year colleges have on-campus housing, but some may not.

Comprehensive College/Upper-Level Colleges

These public or private institutions offer all that a four-year college does, plus graduate (master's) and/or professional programs. They may also offer one or two programs at the doctorate level. Teaching is the primary function of these institutions, although the faculty members are often required to have their own research agendas that along with teaching are part of their job requirements. Many, but not all of these colleges, have on-campus housing.

Universities

These public or private institutions offer all that a comprehensive college or upper-level college does plus a variety of doctoral programs. Research is important to a university and faculty member, and many of these institutions are primarily focused on their research agendas. Most universities offer on-campus and off-campus housing.

Research Universities

A research university has a research focus that is currently classified by the Carnegie Foundation as "heavy" or "very heavy." Scientific research is fundamental to the mission of these universities and to their faculty. Clemson University is an example of a "heavy" research university. Duke, with its large medical campus, is classified as a "very heavy" research university. Research universities often have relationships with U.S. state and federal government agencies, as well as with businesses and industries worldwide to provide researchers and resources for conducting research. Research universities provide a variety of on- and off-campus housing opportunities.

Flagship Universities

Each of the 50 states in the United States has the option to designate one state university as its leading school. In doing so, each state invests more money in that institution than in any other institution in the state, which should improve the quality of that particular institution. For example, the University of Maryland at College Park is "flagship" university of the state of Maryland, and the University of Virginia is Virginia's flagship. This does not necessarily mean that the flagship university is the best university or educational institution in the state, as there are many private schools. All flagship universities will have student housing.

Elite Universities

Elite universities are private institutions that are highly selective and have large endowments (monetary donations). These institutions vary greatly in the size of their student bodies, but consistently charge more than $30,000 per year for tuition. Some examples of elite universities are: **Columbia University** in New York, **Harvard University** in Massachusetts, **Brown University** in Rhode Island, **Yale University** in Connecticut, **Princeton University** in New Jersey, **Dartmouth College** in New Hampshire, the **University of Pennsylvania** in Pennsylvania, Massachusetts Institute of Technology, **Cornell University** in New York, and Stanford University in California. The schools in bold print are Ivy League schools; they are among the oldest institutions in the country.

This is not a fully representative list of all the elite, prestigious, or even the best colleges and universities in the United States. You can visit the *U.S. News & World Report* website to see several lists of how they rank colleges and universities at *www.collegeconfidential.com/college_rankings/USNews.htm*.

Professional Schools

These schools are either part of a university or separate from a university that prepares students for a specific professional level of employment. A national accreditation body generally accredits these schools, and completion of the program allows the student to practice in that field. Law schools, medical schools, schools of psychology, and dental schools are examples of professional schools.

The Application Process and Package

Once you have decided on the college or university that is right for your goals, contact the school and request application information. Many of them have made this process easier by giving access to materials via the Internet: however, requesting an application package by regular mail establishes a more personal correspondence. Many students are surprised by the early application deadlines given for international students, so we advise you to begin this process **at least 18 months to two years before you intend to arrive in the United States to study.** Deadlines for completed applications will be given in the application materials that you request, but by the time you receive the documents, the deadline for the term in which you are interested may have passed. For example, it is not uncommon for the target date for international student applications to be from early January to early March for the fall semester, which usually begins late August or early September. Deadlines for spring admission are often late July or early August for the term beginning sometime in January. Be aware that some schools only admit international students on F-1 student visas to begin in the fall term.

The application package that you will receive can be overwhelming. For some people, the application process can seem so difficult that they drop out right away. It is important that you take an organized approach to completing the application. Be patient. Only then can you finish the paperwork required by the school. Be sure you have provided all of the items that the school has requested to be sent with the application. There is no standard application package for all of the schools in the United States. Each institution sets up its own procedures, and these also vary depending on whether you are applying as an undergraduate or a graduate student. Most schools ask for a *formal application* to be filled out, an *application fee*, some kind of *transcript* or an official record of your previous educational experience, a *formal essay* detailing your goals and achievements, *letters of recommendation,* and *standardized test scores.*

Many colleges and universities take a great deal of pride and are often measured against each other by how selective they are. This means that many schools receive significantly more applications than they can accept, and they can be very particular about whom they choose to be a part of their academic community. American colleges and universities do not have entrance exams like many universities around the world. They often require standardized test scores like the SAT® (Standardized Aptitude Test), and international applicants are asked to take the TOEFL® (Test of English as a Foreign Language). American colleges try to choose the students who have the best grades, have participated in extracurricular activities, and have shown leadership during their secondary school years. Some examples of extracurricular activities are participation on the debate team, playing on a sports team, being a cheerleader, participating in a student organization, or holding an office in student government. This is a very short list, but it is important to present yourself in the application in the best way possible. Don't let an incomplete or poorly done application prevent you from being admitted to the school that you have chosen!

The Application

Applications can be requested in writing, via email, and by downloading from the school's website. Also, it may be possible to complete the application directly online from the institutional website. The application is generally used to collect information about the student. You can be asked to write about yourself and to provide your educational background, statistical information, study plans, and standardized test scores, which must be supported by official records that have been sent directly from each testing service. Most applications require a signature from the student; this holds the student accountable for the information given in the application.

Application Fees

Fees vary from nothing or very little to more than $100. The average fee is around $45. This serves not only as a payment to offset the cost of processing applications, but to limit applications to those who are serious about attending the school. Applying to many schools at one time can become very expensive.

Transcripts

For undergraduates, a formal scholastic record from secondary school is required. This should include your grades, what the grades mean, your final grade point average (GPA), and your date of graduation. If the document cannot be provided in English, an official translation with the original attached should be acceptable. Your application package from the college should indicate what you will specifically need to include to satisfy the documentation of your secondary school records.

For graduate students, your undergraduate transcripts need to be officially translated and certified by a university or government official. Most programs will also require that you have your transcripts officially reviewed by a professional evaluation service in the United States. The school you are applying to will indicate what it expects in terms of transcripts; however, it is recommended that you have your transcripts evaluated. The Appendix (page 186) contains a sample list of evaluation services that you might use.

If you have completed some coursework at a university in your country but have not graduated, it is a good idea to have your transcripts translated and evaluated. You may be able to receive some undergraduate credit for the work you have done that could save you valuable time and money.

The Essay

The essay should be used to highlight the aspects or successes about you and your experience that were not addressed in the overall application. The application usually gives some guidelines about what is expected in the essay, but be sure to take advantage of the opportunity to show who you really are and where you are going in your future. There are many books and websites that give support for writing your essay. Make sure you use your own writing and that what you write is accurate. This website can be useful: *www.collegeboard.com/ student/apply/essay-skills/index.html.*

Letters of Recommendation

Most applications, particularly graduate applications, ask for recommendations (letters of support) from your former professors and other professionals who can evaluate your achievements in academics, extracurricular activities, and community service.

Tests

Most colleges will ask for several standardized test scores. The scores they ask for will differ depending on whether you are applying for graduate or undergraduate study and on the kind of program you plan to enter. The following is a list of the most common tests.

The Test of English as a Foreign Language (TOEFL®)

Most international students must submit an up-to-date TOEFL® score that meets the school's published requirement. (Exceptions are normally made for students from some English-speaking countries like the United Kingdom, Canada, Australia, and New Zealand.) The scores can range from 500 to 600 on the paper TOEFL®, 62 to 76 for the Internet-based test (iBT), and 180 to 210 on the computer-based test (CBT). Graduate programs often ask for higher scores. The TOEFL® is designed to give an indication of whether a student's English language ability is appropriate for successful academic study. Many schools retest students with their own test when students arrive, and some students are placed into ESL courses to complete their language preparation and to support their initial academic study. Some schools will admit students without a TOEFL® score directly into their ESL programs. For specific information about the TOEFL®, visit ETS's website at *www.toefl.org.*

International English Language Testing System (IELTS®)

Some colleges are including the IELTS™ as an alternative to the TOEFL®. This is a test that has been used around the world, particularly to study in the United Kingdom and Australia. For more information on this test go to: *www.ielts.org/*.

The Scholastic Assessment Test (SAT®)/
American College Testing Assessment (ACT®)

The SAT® and the ACT® are standardized tests that most undergraduate programs require of entering freshman (first-year students). These tests measure math, English, reading, science, and writing abilities that require critical-thinking skills. In addition, components that can assess knowledge in subject areas are available and can be required by certain programs. For more information, access:

SAT®: *www.collegeboard.com/student/index.html?student*

ACT®: *www.act.org/*

The Graduate Record Examination (GRE®)

The GRE® is a standardized test used to predict a student's potential for graduate study. It measures verbal, analytical, and quantitative reasoning skills. For more information, access *www.ets.org*.

The Graduate Management Admissions Test (GMAT®)

The GMAT® replaces the GRE® for students who are interested in studying in a Business Administration (MBA) or management program. For more information, access *www.mba.com/mba/TaketheGMAT*.

The Law School Admission Test (LSAT®)

The LSAT replaces the GRE® and GMAT® for students interested in studying at a law school. For more information, access *www.lsat-center.com/lsat-page1.html*.

All in all, be advised that the SAT®, ACT®, GRE®, GMAT®, and LSAT® were designed for native English speakers and that the complicated language structures can make them extra difficult for non-native English speakers.

Visas, Visas!

You cannot just jump on a plane and begin studying in a degree program in the United States. Getting into the country can be very difficult because of strict laws regulating entry. You must also apply to the U.S. government for a visa appropriate to the program of study you have chosen. The school to which you are applying will provide you with a list of requirements that will be needed to complete your visa application. Both the admission application and the paperwork for your visa application are generally done at the same time. However, the visa application process is not finalized until the school has accepted you and has issued the appropriate documents and until a formal application for a visa at the U.S. Embassy or Consulate in your country has been successfully completed.

A list of important documents and terms related to visas includes:

- **Passport.** This document issued by your government identifies you as a national of your country and permits you to travel outside of your country. A passport must always be kept valid. If you lose your passport or if it expires while you are outside of your country, go to your embassy immediately and get a replacement. Always keep photocopies of all of your documents related to your passport, visa, and any other official documents in a safe and secure place.

- **Travel Document.** A person who is not a national of a particular country but who resides in that country can be issued a travel document, usually called a **Certificate of Identity** that will enable the person to travel.

- **Visas.** A visa is a stamp placed in the passport that gives you permission to enter a particular country. A visa stamp issued by the U.S. Embassy or Consulate should be viewed like an entrance ticket that can be used over and over until it expires. Many people are confused by what a visa does. In short, it lets you into the country.

- **Visa Status**. When a person arrives at a *port of entry* such as an airport, a border crossing, or a seaport in the United States, they are subject to inspection by an officer from the U.S. Department of Homeland Security (DHS). The DHS inspector will carefully examine your passport, visa, and any supporting documents related to

---

☆ A Useful Tip

Admission to an ESL program does not mean that the student has been accepted into that institution's academic programs. Most English language institutes (ELIs) or intensive English programs (IEPs) issue "Language Study" I-20s. ESL students generally have to go through the same competitive application process as other students. Some students are surprised when they are not admitted to a university after completing very expensive ESL programs. However, most schools that do issue I-20s for ESL have a very clearly articulated path for students to enter their academic programs and to process a "Level Change" I-20 with the U.S. Department of Homeland Security.

your visa. If everything is in order, the inspector will then confer a valid visa status based on the visa stamp in the passport. The visa status is indicated on a small white card called a Form I-94. Most international entries, including diplomats, receive an I-94. The airlines give each passenger a blank form, and it's processed at the port of entry. This document is very important because it identifies your status and indicates how long you are allowed to stay in the United States.

☆ A Useful Tip

Although your visa stamp can expire while you are in the United States, your I-94 card must not expire. If you think that you are going to exceed the date on your I-94 card, you should apply for an extension with the DHS. The DHS may or may not grant an extension depending on the reasons you give and the terms of your visa. You—not the school or your hosts—are solely responsible for maintaining your visa status.

Once you are admitted into the United States and have a valid I-94, your visa stamp in your passport is no longer important. It only will become significant again if you leave the United States. You will then need a valid visa to re-enter the United States, and you will once again be conferred status at the port of entry by a DHS inspector through an I-94 card. Your visa status is valid as long as is indicated on the Form I-94. The date stamped on the I-94 becomes the most important date in your entry documentation. You can lose your visa status if you are found to have violated the terms of your visa. You will then have to either apply to the DHS for a reinstatement of your visa status, or leave the country voluntarily.

Many different kinds of visas permit individuals to request entry into the United States. For information concerning visa categories not listed, or for more details about those that are listed, contact the U.S. Embassy or Consulate in your country. The following represents some of the most common temporary visas.

Visa Waiver Program (VWP)

The visa waiver program allows visitors who qualify from 27 countries to enter the United States without a visa for a period of 90 days. The term *waiver* means that a visa in the traveler's passport is not needed. This period of stay cannot be extended or changed to another status. The traveler must have a machine-readable passport that is valid for six months past the intended date of departure. The 27 countries are: Andorra, Australia, Austria, Belgium, Brunei, Denmark, Finland, France, Germany, Iceland, Ireland, Italy, Japan, Liechtenstein, Luxembourg, Monaco, The Netherlands, New Zealand, Norway,

Portugal, Singapore, San Marino, Slovenia, Spain, Sweden, Switzerland, and the United Kingdom.* The VWP is for visiting purposes only, and individuals cannot study or work while in the United States. It would be appropriate for someone to visit different schools and gather information about a school and its application procedures, but the visa application would have to be made by the student in his or her home country. Do not enter the United States under this program if you intend to study! For more information and updates, go to the Visa Waver Program on the U.S. Department of State site: *http://travel.state.gov.*

Visitor's Visa (B1/B2)

The B visa category is for people who want to visit the United States for a period of six months or less. Through application directly to the local Department of Homeland Security office, it is possible to extend this status for an additional six months. The B-1 category is for visitors who are in the United States for business or employment outside of their own country. The B-2 category is for tourist purposes. Individuals who enter in B visa status are not eligible for employment or study within the country. Therefore, this visa is not appropriate for students who intend to study in the United States.

Once an individual is in the U.S. on a B2 visa, it is possible, but not a guarantee, to change "visa status" to F-1 Student. A person with a valid B visa should work with the International Student Office at the college or university he or she wishes to attend to process a Change of Status Application. If a B visa holder's application for a Change of Status is approved by the U.S. Citizenship and Immigration Services, then a full-time course of study can be pursued. It should be noted that a visa is not issued with the Approval of Change of Status. If a person changes his or her visa status within the United States and then leaves the country for any reason, he or she must apply for a new visa to re-enter the United States.

Exchange Visitor Visa (J-1)

This type of visa may be appropriate for certain students and scholars—particularly those sponsored by agencies, foundations, the U.S. government, or their home governments. The purpose of this visa is for cultural and intellectual exchange. It is granted by presenting a Certificate of Eligibility (Form DS-2019) and supporting financial documentation from a sponsoring agency. The accompanying dependents of a J-1 Exchange Visitor (a spouse and a child, for example) enter the U. S. on a J-2 visa that may, in some cases, permit employment with approval of the U.S. Department of Homeland Security. Children

---

*This information is accurate as of May 5, 2007.

who hold J-2 visas can attend public elementary and secondary schools. J-2 visa holders that meet post-secondary admissions requirements are able to study full-time. It is important to note that in many cases, Exchange Visitors must leave the United States at the conclusion of their programs and may not change their visa statuses until a two-year home country residence has been completed. For more detailed information on J visas, go to *http://travel.state.gov;* follow the links to the Exchange Visitor (J) Visas.

Student Visas (F-1)

The F-1 visa is the appropriate visa for a student to obtain to study full-time in the United States. To enter the United States, international students will need a passport from their government, a visa from the U.S. Consulate, and a properly endorsed Form I-20 with supporting documents from a school. At the port of entry, a student will present to the INS inspector an I-20 with supporting documents and a passport with a valid F-1 visa. On successful inspection, F-1 visa status is granted when the inspector stamps the Form I-20 and Form I-94 with an entry date and endorses both the I-94 with the initials D/S. More detailed information on the F-1 visa is available from *www.usastudentvisa.org.*

To apply for a Student (F-1) or Exchange (J-1) visa, a passport and a Certificate of Eligibility (Form I-20 for F-1 and Form DS-2019 for J-1) are needed along with supporting financial documentation (see pages 33–35). A Form I-20 or DS-2019 will be issued to a student once he or she is admitted to the college or university and has shown adequate financial support will be provided. A student on an F-1 visa must enroll for at least 12 credits each semester in an undergraduate academic program, 9 hours in a graduate program, or at least 18 contact hours in an intensive ESL program. There are strict regulations concerning students studying on F-1 and J-1 visas, and a student on an F-1 visa should be prepared not to work for the first academic year.

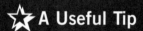 **A Useful Tip**

D/S represents "duration of status," which means that the individual will remain in status as long as he or she holds a valid I-20, is pursuing a full course of study, and has complied with the regulatory terms or rules of the F-1 visa.

Dependent(s) of F-1 (F-2)

The F-2 visa is granted to the spouse or children of an F-1 visa student. Individuals on F-2 visas are not eligible for full-time study at colleges or universities in the United States. Children on F-2 visas can access public schools without tuition and would pay the same fees, if any, as any other family living in the community. Individuals on F-2 visas **are not permitted** to work in the United States. Unauthorized employment would be considered a violation of the F-2 visa status.

F-1 Student and J-1 Exchange Visa Application

The school that you decide to attend must have the ability to issue Form I-20s if you are seeking an F-1 visa, and it must be able to issue Form DS-2019 for J-1 visas. These are two different programs, and some schools may only be eligible to issue one of the forms. The application package that you receive should have a checklist of the papers you need to have prepared in order to qualify for an I-20 or a DS-2019. Schools are required to estimate the total cost of being a student for an academic year, including tuition, fees, living expenses, books, supplies, and medical insurance. International students must be able to show that there are sufficient funds available for study at that financial level.

✓ **Finances.** A school that issues I-20s and DS-2019s should include a list of costs in the application package. It will look like the following sample:

Tuition and mandatory fees: (two semesters)	$12,000
Living expenses for 12 months (includes room, board, local transportation, and incidental costs)	$11,000
Books and supplies	$900
Medical insurance	$800
Total	**$24,700**

Before the school issues you an I-20 or a DS-2019, you will need to present documentation that shows that you have access to personal or family funds or through sponsors that can cover $24,700 for the year, the sample school estimate. (Of course, the dollar figure will vary depending on the school and its location.) This can be done through a variety of ways, such as a bank statement showing sufficient funds from your own account. If someone is sponsoring your schooling, he or she must provide a **sworn affidavit of support** (an official declaration) that includes a bank statement showing funds to cover the expenses; or a letter from an employer showing a high enough salary; or tax returns from a business, stock portfolios, or any combination of the above. The school will be very clear with you about what it is looking for and will provide any official documents you will need.

Finally, once you have carefully completed your application and provided all of the required support material, all you need do is wait and hope for the best. You might receive a letter requesting more specific information than you had originally sent. If so, you should respond immediately. You might receive a rejection letter stating that the school is highly competitive and you were not accepted. If so, perhaps one of the other schools you applied to will accept you.

⭐ A Useful Tip

When you go to the interview, you should have your study plan ready, know your goals, and know why you want to study abroad. Also, you should be prepared to be photographed and to have sample fingerprints taken.

If you receive a letter of acceptance, keep it in a safe place. You will need to show the acceptance letter to the embassy or consulate. Your acceptance package should either include your I-20 or DS-2019, or should let you know that it will be sent to you soon.

Once you receive a full acceptance package from your school, you are now almost ready to approach the U.S. Embassy or Consulate to request an F-1 or J-1 visa. The first thing you must do is pay your SEVIS I-901 Fee. SEVIS is the system that the United States government uses to monitor international students on J and F visas. A fee of $100 is required of all applicants.

A summary of SEVIS can be found on pages 35–36. Once you have received the receipt for your I-901 fee, call to find out the appropriate procedures for your embassy or consulate. It varies from country to country. However, most require that you come in person for an interview with an official in the visa section.

You should bring:

- ✓ a $100 visa application fee
- ✓ a completed Form DF156 (blank forms are available at the U.S. Consular Offices)
- ✓ a photograph 37 × 37 mm showing your full face without head-covering
- ✓ an acceptance letter and your Form I-20 or DS-2019
- ✓ any supporting financial documents, which should be less than six months old, and evidence that shows that you plan to return to your home country

One of the most common reasons for a visa denial is that the student failed to demonstrate appropriate ties to his or her home country such as a residence (apartment, home), other property, a job, or strong family ties. The inspecting officer may ask for more documentation, deny your visa, or grant a visa immediately following your interview. If the embassy official asks for more documentation, provide it as quickly as possible. If your visa application is denied, the inspecting official should tell you why your application is being denied. Inform your advisor at the school to see if he or she can help to determine if anything can be done to address the denial. In most cases, there is not much that can be done other than to try again at a later date.

After your visa is granted, there is a lot to be done to prepare for your arrival in the United States.

SEVIS (the Student and Exchange Visitor Information System)

The U.S. government and colleges and universities are partners in bringing students to study in the United States. Multiple agencies are involved in the process. SEVIS is the system used to archive and communicate information about F-1 and J-1 students. The SEVIS website *(www.ice.gov/SEVIS)* has detailed information about the system and states that "SEVIS was activated in 2003 to track and monitor the status and activities of non-immigrant and exchange visitors who enter the United States. This web-based system collects real-time information on non-immigrant students and exchange visitors and shares it with other governmental agencies."

A **Designated School Official (DSO),** who is an employee at the college or university, has access to SEVIS. When an I-20 or a DS-2019 is created by a college or university, a SEVIS file is generated. This is called an **initial** SEVIS file. When a student has an interview for a visa application at the U.S. Embassy or Consulate, the officials there have access to the student's SEVIS file, and they are able to view and enter information. If a visa is issued, it is noted in the student's SEVIS file. When the student enters the United States, a DHS official at the port of entry also has access to the student's SEVIS file and can view and enter information. After the student is granted entry into the country, the student should report as soon as possible to the institution indicated on his or her I-20 or DS-2019. Once the student is registered and enrolled in classes, he or she becomes **active** in SEVIS and is considered to be **in status.** SEVIS is used by the school to keep student information updated and to report any special permissions, exceptions, or violations related to visa status. For example, if a student has legitimate and documented medical problems that interrupt his or her ability to study, this information is entered into SEVIS, so the visa status is maintained. In addition, if a student does not maintain a full-time load of classes, this information is entered into SEVIS. Then the student must apply for a reinstatement of visa status or leave the country.

We cannot stress enough how important it is for you to understand what is expected to maintain your visa status. You are held responsible for complying with the terms of your visa, and non-compliance is immediately reported. Most students do not have any problems, so they are successful in achieving their educational goal. If you have questions, do not hesitate to meet with the International Student Advisor on your campus.

CHAPTER 3

Newcomer's Checklist

> *A*t the end of Chapter 2, you were leaving the U.S. Embassy or Consulate with a new visa in your passport. At this point, you have been accepted by the school of your choice, verified your acceptance, received the appropriate forms from the school and your sponsors, and have successfully secured a visa to request entry into the United States. What should you do next?

Now, are you ready to fly? Has the Foreign Student Advisor of your school requested your travel itinerary?

Make sure that you take all the visa paperwork and your passport on the plane with you. You should also have your supporting financial documentation used to secure your visa, your admission letter, and the SEVIS fee receipt. These documents will be needed immediately when you arrive at the U.S. airport. Keep them on your person, and do not put them in the baggage you plan to check. This will cause an unnecessary delay at the port of entry. Arrive at the airport at least two hours early for international flights. The entry processing, customs, and baggage check can take time.

Many schools will provide transportation from the airport if they know when you are arriving. If your school does not provide this service, do you know where you need to go when you arrive and how you are going to get there? Try to make these arrangements in advance, if possible. Check the airport shuttle (van) services on the airport's website. Shuttles are often less expensive than taxis, especially if you are traveling far from the airport.

Dates

The first thing you should do is to check the dates that the school indicates are important. A **reporting date** is entered on your I-20 or DS 2019, and you must report to the International Student Advisor before that date. This is normally much earlier than the first day of classes. Most schools will have an orientation for incoming international students, and you should be there to participate.

Also, you need to know the date when you can enter your dormitory or other form of housing. If you arrive too early, you will have to arrange for temporary housing.

Knowing all of these dates will help you to decide when you need to arrive in the United States. Buy your airplane ticket early because if you wait too long, it may be more difficult to fly on the date of your choice. Make sure that you forward any required deposits needed to secure your admission or dorm room.

> ## ⭐ An Important Note
>
> You will not be permitted to enter the United States more than 30 days before your reporting date.

Quarantine

Several weeks before your travel, check with the U.S. Embassy and the airline you are traveling with concerning any quarantine, import/export restrictions, or immunization requirements pertinent to exiting your country and entering the United States.

In-Flight Documentation

While you are in flight to the United States, you will be asked to fill out two important documents. One is called CF-6059 Customs Declaration Form; it identifies any items you are bringing in the country that may need to be taxed or identified for inspection. The other is an I-94 Arrival-Departure Record Form. Form I-94 will become an important part of your visa documentation and will eventually be stapled into your passport. Both forms should be filled out carefully in your best handwriting. They will be presented with the rest of your visa paperwork at your initial inspection.

Inspection

When you arrive at the airport in the United States, you will be at a port of entry. You must go through inspection of your visa paperwork by the U.S. Department of Homeland Security's Bureau of Customs and Border Protection and request entry into the United States. The inspector will open the sealed envelope that was attached to your passport at the embassy, review the documents you have provided to support your I-20 or DS 2019, review your SEVIS record, and take your fingerprints and a photo. The inspector will also ask a few questions related to your entry into the United States. Answer the questions clearly and honestly.

If your paperwork is correct, the inspector will enter your arrival information into SEVIS and into a system called the Arrival and Departure Information System (ADIS). Your passport, your I-20 or DS 2019, and the Form I-94 you filled out on the airplane during your flight will be stamped with an entry date. For F-1 visa holders, your I-94 and I-20 will be marked with the letters D/S, which represents Duration of Status. D/S means that you are allowed to stay as long as you are maintaining your status and are enrolled in a full course of study. For J-1 visa holders, D/S is normally indicated on the I-94 and DS 2019, but it is also possible that a date will be entered based on the program completion date. You must initially attend the school that is indicated on your stamped I-20 or DS 2019. If you attend another institution, you have violated your visa and you are out-of-status (See Maintaining Your Visa Status, pages 43–44). It is possible to transfer schools after attending one complete term at the school on the I-20 or DS 2019, but be careful to follow the appropriate transfer procedures.

Transferring

Students sometimes select a college or university for a variety of reasons, they discover that they may have more success at another institution. It is possible to transfer from the initial school on your SEVIS record to another school; however, you must plan very carefully for this. First, you must have an acceptance letter from the new institution. Next, you must be "in status" and in good standing at your current school. You should work with the ISA at the school you are leaving and with the school you are transferring to for assistance in transferring your SEVIS and academic records. Each school will have other forms specific to it that you will also need to complete.

As of August 2007, the DHS clarified that it is possible to transfer schools even if you haven't attended the initial school on your SEVIS record. It is important to note, however, that you must report to the school listed on your I-20. This can be done in person, by telephone, email, or fax. Also, you must already be accepted at the new school, and the start date of the new school must be within 30 days of your entry into the United Stages. The details for this transfer can be found at *www.ice.gov/sevis/f_1_transfer.htm.*

After the inspection, get your baggage and pass through customs. This is where you must declare any taxable property you are carrying and where your baggage may be inspected for any substances that are not allowed to be brought in the United States, such as plants, food or food products, or illegal drugs.

After passing through customs, you enter the airport terminal and meet your ride or proceed to the public transportation area. Be careful of any stranger at the airport, who offers you help you didn't ask for or asks for personal information. You should proceed to your temporary or permanent housing from the airport in order to safely store your luggage and to rest from your travels. International flights can take a great deal of energy out of you.

Requirements Related to the School

Reporting

You should report to the **International (or Foreign) Student Advisor (ISA)** as soon as possible after arriving in the United States. The ISA works for the school, not for the U.S. Department of Homeland Security or the U.S. State Department. ISAs are responsible for advising students concerning the laws and regulations of their visa and to ensure that the school follows the regulations related to the privilege of issuing Forms I-20 and DS 2019 for study in the United States. Any questions that you may have concerning your visa or visa status should always be directed to the ISA.

Bring your passport, Form I-94, and stamped I-20 or DS 2019 with you to your meeting with the ISA. The ISA will make photocopies of these documents. Your ISA is an important contact; be sure to ask him or her questions about anything you do not understand. If the ISA cannot answer your questions, you will be directed to the appropriate office at your school. Your ISA should let you know what you need to do next. The ISA will tell you about the orientation meetings you should attend and about any registration deadlines. Your ISA may also tell you about any placement tests you need to take before you register. Make certain that you take any required placement tests, usually for Math and English, as these will determine your ability to register for classes. Your ISA will also direct you to your assigned academic advisor or to an academic counselor concerning academic matters.

Academic Advisor/Academic Counseling

Students on an I-20 specifically related to English language training are often advised within the ESL or intensive English program (IEP). For academic study, students are required to meet with an Academic Advisor, who is usually a faculty member in your major field, or an Academic Counselor, who is a professional trained in advising students about their academic program. Given the wide range of choices available to students, academic advising and counseling are very helpful to guide students along the long road to graduation. Colleges and universities in many countries do not provide this service because the curriculum is generally set: Every student is given a particular schedule of classes that he or she should take. In the United States, more responsibility is placed on students for making choices concerning their classes and degrees. It's important for you to make a plan with your advisor. Remember, there are many interesting classes offered at your school, but do not waste time taking too many classes that are not related to the degree that you are seeking.

Also, try to familiarize yourself with the schedule of classes and the basic requirements of your major. You should be able to work out the classes that you plan to take during the meeting with your advisor. Be sure to have the advisor sign off on your choices so that you can register. Students studying on F-1 and J-1 visas are required to register for a full-time load. This is generally 12 or more undergraduate credit hours, 9 or more graduate hours, or 18 or more contact hours in an IEP.

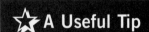

A Useful Tip

It is your responsibility to register for a full-time course load. If you fail to register for a full-time load, then your visa will be labeled out-of-status. It is a good idea to check with your ISA after you have registered to confirm that you have correctly registered for a full load.

Registering for Classes

Registration involves more than just selecting your classes with an advisor or an academic counselor. First, there is the physical process of submitting your registration and paying your tuition. For some colleges, this is done via a specific office or by mail. For many schools this now can be done via the telephone or the Internet. After you have submitted your schedule request, you may receive a written confirmation and a bill. Learn more about registration and payment procedures in your college or university from the school's website, and be sure to pay your tuition and fees on time. Some schools expect you to pay immediately after registering. Check with your ISA or a counselor for the correct procedures.

Housing

Your acceptance package should include an application for housing with a request for a deposit that can be several hundred dollars. Take care to pay this as early as possible. If the school does not offer housing, you should arrive early enough to secure a place to live. Off-campus housing can vary in quality and price. Make sure you give yourself enough time to make a careful selection. Rents for a one-room apartment (often called a single or an efficiency) can range from $400 per month in rural areas to more than $1,900 per month in a large city. A security deposit and the first and last month's rent are often required. The security deposit is used to repair any damage to the property above and beyond what is expected from normal living. If you take care of the property, most of this deposit is returned. Most rentals require the signing of a lease, which is a contract to stay for a specific period (normally for one year). Be careful and get help, if possible. Your ISA at the college can be very helpful in guiding your housing selection. Do not be afraid to ask for assistance.

Insurance

Health insurance allows you to get professional medical help according to the particular rules and conditions that your insurance plan contains. Health insurance is required for international students at most schools. Many schools require you to use the school's insurance policy or one that meets or exceeds the coverage (available services) of the school's policy. Your school will inform you of any immunizations that you will need and of the ways in which you will need to document that you have received the immunizations. It may be more comfortable for you to get these shots from your own doctor before coming to the United States, but if you do, make sure you get the appropriate documentation. There may be immunizations that are required before you enter the United States. These requirements differ from country to country, so you are well advised to check with the U.S. Embassy or consulate in your home country for details.

> ### ☆ A Useful Tip
>
> You absolutely must have medical insurance. Medical costs in the United States can be very expensive, even for a minor visit to a doctor or hospital. Even if the school does not require that you get medical insurance, get it anyway!

Many students have found out how expensive health care can be in the United States by having to interrupt or even end their studies because a large medical bill has taken their funds. Get medical insurance; do not get caught in a compromising financial situation because you did not purchase insurance.

A Note about ESL

Usually, your TOEFL® score accurately represents your ability to use the English language. Some students, however, are surprised when they receive a low-level placement after taking an ESL placement test at the school. The students often feel that they could have done better if they had had more time for the test. Time indeed is an important factor of most placement tests. Quite often students make wrong judgments about how well they can communicate in English. In addition, some students often have an inflated (exaggerated) sense of their English proficiency. Do not be upset if you are placed at a lower level than you expected. If you are really placed in the wrong level, the teacher will notice, and most programs have a way to move students in the first week. However, you should not expect to be moved up a level just because you want to move. If you are placed in a level that is too high, you will not learn as much and you will become a burden on the students that belong in the class. ESL programs maintain their quality by being careful to accurately place students in the appropriate levels and by moving them efficiently and effectively through the levels.

It is extremely important that you have the appropriate English language skills to handle college-level instruction. Struggling with the language and the content of a course at the same time can put a student far behind the rest of the class. If you have a problem with English, get help either through an ESL program, the academic counseling center, the college tutoring center, or the college reading and writing center. Any of these offices should be able to direct you to a source of help. Also, many community or adult education programs offer ESL classes that can help.

Maintaining Your Visa Status

As indicated in Chapter 2, there is a distinction between a visa and visa status. The U.S. Department of State issues visas at the U.S. Embassy or consulate in your country. A visa allows you to enter the United States to request admittance from the U.S. Department of Homeland Security at the port of entry. The U.S. Department of Homeland Security allows you to enter the country upon inspection and updates your SEVIS record. Your visa status is established when you report to the school and register for classes. At that time an official at the college or university enters information into your SEVIS record and your record becomes "active."

You should be very clear concerning the regulations related to your visa. These vary between F-1 and J-1 visas. Basically, you can maintain your status by always registering for a full-time load of classes, by attending classes and doing the work required by the professor, by making sure that your paperwork is kept up-to-date, and by not getting a job without the U.S. Department of

Homeland Security's approval. (Though opportunities are very limited, some students can get on-campus employment for 20 hours or less per week.) This is a very simple list. To obtain a more detailed list, meet with your ISA.

If you become ill or if you are having trouble in your class, you must communicate immediately with your ISA. The ISA can be of help and give you the support you might need to get through a difficult time and still maintain your visa status. If someone gives you advice that makes you confused or uncomfortable, discuss it with your ISA before taking the advice. For example, if you are having difficulty in a class and the professor recommends that dropping or withdrawing from a course might be helpful, meet immediately with your ISA! If withdrawing from a course takes you below a full-time course load, your visa will be labeled out-of–status. If you are determined to be out-of-status by your ISA, then you must either return home or go through a complicated paperwork process that involves making a formal request to the U.S. Department of Homeland Security for a reinstatement of your visa status. This process requires a detailed explanation of why you were unable to meet the requirements of your visa. Do not expect to be automatically granted a reinstatement. You must convince the Department of Homeland Security that there was a good reason (just cause) for falling out-of-status.

Employment

Employment regulations for J-1 visa holders are based on the terms of the program. J-1 students should meet with their ISAs to be clear about those terms. F-1 students are not eligible for off-campus employment during their first academic year (nine months, fall and spring semesters). Regulations allow for work on campus; however, F-1 students should meet with their ISAs to determine employment eligibility and authorization procedures before accepting any employment. As stated, on-campus employment opportunities are extremely limited, and F-1 status does not guarantee employment. After a student has completed one academic year of study, there are possibilities for employment off campus. You should discuss the possibility of off-campus employment with your ISA and under no circumstances should you accept any job without careful and direct consultation with your ISA.

Social Security Number/ Tax Identification Number

This is usually a very confusing area for international students. From the Social Security Administration's (SSA) point of view, a social security number (SSN) is used for employment purposes only and is not a national identity number. An SSN is not required for securing a bank account or getting a driver's license. But in reality, unfortunately, not having an SSN can make life difficult for an international student because many institutions in the United States do not interpret the SSA's explanation about a social security number correctly. According to regulations, only those F-1 and J-1 students who are authorized for employment and have a job offer can receive an SSN. Students who are not authorized for work should receive a Tax Identification Number (TIN). A TIN functions in much the same way as an SSN and can be used in place of an SSN. For example, when you apply for a lease on an apartment, get a credit card, or buy a car, you may be asked for an SSN. A TIN should satisfy any of these requests. It is important that you protect your SSN or ITIN. Do not share it with anyone that is clearly not an official. If you are unsure about giving it, ask your ISA. Your SSN or ITIN can be used by someone else to make false applications, for example bank accounts or credit cards. This is called "identity theft." All students on F-1 and J-1 visas must file a tax return by using the IRS Form 1040NR whether you have worked or not. See your ISA concerning general filing requirements.

American Law

One thing that strikes international students once they have arrived is that although the United States is known as "the land of the free," there seem to be a lot of rules to follow and many signs that go with those rules! During a seminar, one student exclaimed, "Everywhere I turn I either see the word *no* or *don't* attached to a rule!" Well, the student is correct. The United States does give its citizens a great deal of political freedom, but along with that goes personal responsibility. There are many laws that govern social behavior that you must become aware of before you unknowingly break the law. "I did not know about this law," some students say. Unknowingly breaking the law is not an excuse that will hold up in a court of law. The easiest laws to break for any student have to do with two major responsibilities: drinking alcoholic beverages and owning and operating a car.

A Case to Think About

Albert had a difficult but successful day on campus. He registered for classes, paid tuition and fees, and had a whole evening ahead of him free. He stopped by a convenience store and bought a bottle of beer. The weather was hot and humid, and he decided to sit down near the store and drink his beer. He found a place on a curb—happy and relaxed—and opened the bottle. In a few minutes, a police car pulled next to him.

"Do you know what you are doing now?" asked the officer.

"Yes, I am drinking beer," replied Albert smiling. "Is anything wrong with it? It is just a beer . . . ."

Yes, there was something wrong in Albert's case. In the state where it happened, drinking alcohol from opened bottles in public places is considered an offense. Because of this seemingly minor episode, Albert's future as a student was now in serious jeopardy.

College life does not take place exclusively in the classroom. College is a time when many students experience life for the first time outside the direct control of their parents. For some students, this newly found freedom is an opportunity to come into their own and show how they can responsibly manage their lives. For others, it is an opportunity to test their personal limits; unfortunately, this results in some kind of problem from an inability to keep up with the work required in class to direct conflict with the police. The role of alcohol and drugs on college campuses is an area of hot debate, and one cannot view a college or a university as a sanctuary from the rules that govern a civil society. Be careful! International students are no different from any other students as far as the law is concerned.

Story . . .

This story was told to us by a faculty member at a large institution.

One day while I was grading papers, I looked out my window and saw a police officer pulling over a very nice sports car. The car was sleek and flashy and looked like it could go very fast. The police officer got out of his car, and he seemed to be quite upset. The driver of the car was smiling as if he didn't care much about what was going on. His smile vanished as the police officer invited him outside and placed him in handcuffs. The driver was then taken away by another officer. The arresting officer then removed the license tags from the vehicle, searched it completely, and had it towed. There was clearly a big difference between what the driver of the car thought was going to happen to him and what the police officer did.

It is important to take time to understand your new environment and your role in it. The college, the community surrounding the college, or the law simply do not tolerate certain types of behavior. Consider drinking. There are severe penalties for driving while intoxicated (DWI) or driving while under the influence of drugs (DUI) that can affect your stay in the United States and the rest of your life. You should be careful even if you are not driving a car, as there are strict laws that regulate over-consumption and underage drinking. Most states set the legal age to drink alcoholic beverages at 21. Any violation of these laws may cause serious consequences, including deportation (removal) from the country.

There will be many opportunities to enjoy college life. There is always something to do, and much of it does not involve drinking alcoholic beverages. It will be easy to avoid the problems surrounding alcohol abuse on campus by making wise choices. Much of this involves those you choose to associate with. Choose your friends wisely and have fun. For many, the friends you make in college will be your friends for life! Don't mess it up by challenging the law or rules, and even worse, getting hurt or hurting someone else.

Getting a Driver's License

If you are going to drive in the United States, you will need to get a driver's license from the state in which you reside, even if you have an international driver's license. Driving in the United States is a very important responsibility, and you can easily get into trouble if you do not completely understand the traffic laws. You must have your driver's license, your vehicle registration, and proof of insurance in your vehicle at all times when you are driving. To get a driver's license, call the nearest state motor vehicle office (Department of Motor Vehicles/Secretary of State Office) and find out what is required to get a license. Your ISA can provide you with this information. Generally, you will be required to take a written test, a driving test, and have your vision (ability to see) tested. You should bring your passport, your I-20 or DS 2019, and a letter that verifies you are a student from your school. You will have to pay a fee as well.

Buying a Car

Having a car can be expensive, and it is a serious responsibility. Owning a car in the United States involves a surprising number of steps. Buying a car can be a difficult and confusing process. Most of us do not know much about cars, even if we drive one every day. It is hard to be sure when you are getting a good deal on a car, and everyone wants a good deal, right? New car prices are normally not fixed and often are deliberately inflated (raised) to allow for some negotiation of the price. Sometimes people will tell you that they have "been taken" or deceived when they were buying a car. This is called "buyer's remorse." These feelings are the result of the vagueness related to buying a car.

Do a great deal of research before buying a new car. If you are buying a new car, visit as many different car dealerships as possible to compare prices. Also, find out what other people have paid for their cars, and ask them for advice or help. Make sure that you are clear about all of the charges the dealership attempts to impose, and question any that seem to be too high or unnecessary. Car dealerships and car-buying services that have fixed prices are becoming more and more popular. You may want to find out which particular automakers offer fixed pricing, which means the price cannot be negotiated, and compare their prices to other dealerships.

There are leasing options that do not require you to purchase the car. Leasing means that you use a car for two or three years and then return it to the dealer. Sometimes leasing is a better option than purchasing. Be careful of hidden costs in leases that are connected to mileage.

In all cases make sure that you understand all of the details involved in your purchase or lease, and be sure to read the whole contract. Only by reading the contract will you find the details that may be unattractive to the buyer.

Getting a loan to pay for a new car may be difficult. You should try to go to your own bank (in the United States) to get a low-interest loan, but do not be surprised or offended if they do not give you a loan. You may not have been in the country long enough to have established a credit history (proof you can pay), which banks rely on to make loan decisions. You may have better luck at the dealership, but do not get caught up in a high-interest loan.

Check with your ISA to find out what support the school provides students in understanding the process of buying or leasing a new car. Some ISA offices offer orientation programs that cover this, or they may have prepared a guide to help you. Lease Agreements and Purchase Contracts are complicated and bind you to a financial commitment. If it is at all possible, bring someone who is familiar with purchasing a car to the dealership to clarify the documents you will be asked to sign. If you know someone, but he or she cannot come with you to the dealership, ask the dealer to allow you to take the paperwork home for review. Another possibility is that some dealerships have staff members on hand that speak languages other than English. You should make some calls and ask if a dealership offers support in your language. Make sure that you fully understand the terms of the documents that you sign.

Buying a new car or leasing one may not be your best options. A new car loses value as soon as you drive it off of the dealer's lot. And you do not generally buy a car at the end of a lease—without paying a lot more money. Therefore, buying a used car is often a good option. However, if you find a used car that you are seriously considering buying, we advise you to have the car inspected by an auto mechanic to ensure the car is working properly. It is worth the money to have an expert assess the car. You do not want to buy someone else's problem or a car that has been wrecked and repaired for a quick sale. Ask your ISA to recommend a good mechanic. A good used car can be reliable transportation. Make sure that you receive a receipt and the Certificate of Title for the vehicle and that the previous owner properly signs over the title to you. The title is the legal certificate of ownership of the vehicle.

When you purchase a car, you must get the car licensed for the state in which you reside. To do this you normally have to pay a tax on the value of the car and a fee. Also, you will be required to get the car officially inspected at an authorized location, which is usually a gas/service station officially certified by the state. If you buy a new car, most of this is done for you at the dealership. If you buy a used car, you have to take care of the legal details yourself. You can get a list of the required paper work from the State's Department of Motor Vehicles in the state you live in. This information is provided on most state websites. Study the legal requirements of the state in which you live that apply to keeping your vehicle legal. Many states require annual (yearly) inspections and emissions testing, and some cities and counties require local stickers for which you must pay a fee.

Once you purchase a car, you must get automobile insurance. This is a requirement. Many students do not consider this in their financial planning; however, automobile insurance can be expensive. For a new car, the monthly insurance payment can be as much as the car payment: from $100 to $200 per month and even higher for young, single adults. Nevertheless, the consequences of not having auto insurance in an accident can ruin your life and the other people's lives who may also be involved in an accident.

Banking in the United States

You should establish your own bank account at a U.S. bank as soon as possible after arriving. You do not need an SSN or a TIN to establish a bank account, but you should bring your passport, your I-20 or DS 2019, and a letter from the school verifying admission. If a bank insists on an SSN, go to another bank. If you cannot find a bank that will start an account for you, go to the local Social Security office and report your experience. That office will give you a letter to take to the bank explaining the current law. Many colleges and universities have a bank on the campus that can take care of your needs. Report persistent problems to the ISA, and he or she can contact the bank on your behalf.

⭐ A Useful Tip

Do not share a bank account with a friend. There are too many unpleasant stories to tell about what has happened to other people in such situations. There is absolutely no need to put your money in someone else's account. Get your own account.

Many types of accounts are available. The most common are **checking** and **savings** accounts, or a combined version of these. Checking accounts keep the day-to-day cash that you need. They generally carry little or no interest, which is a percentage of money you receive back based on how much you keep in the bank. Savings accounts carry a higher percentage of interest (where you earn money just by keeping money in the bank), but there are limits on the number of transactions. Fees are applied if you withdraw money often. Combined accounts are interest-bearing checking accounts that generally carry more interest than checking accounts but less than a savings account. Some types of accounts offer higher interest rates than savings accounts, but they often carry early withdrawal penalties or risk if they are based on investments in the stock market. Be careful to understand the terms of your accounts.

The bank may charge fees for not maintaining a particular balance in your account or for writing more than a certain number of checks per month. Once again, read the fine print in your bank agreement. Also, there may be charges connected to using automatic teller machines (ATM or money machines), including when you make a purchase using your ATM card at a store.

Credit Cards

The use of credit cards is very popular in the United States. They are a convenient way to make purchases and monitor your spending and are often required for securing services like rental cars and hotel rooms. They carry with them the responsibility of using them wisely and not spending beyond your ability to pay. It is a good idea to get a Visa or a MasterCard in your own country before you come to the United States. If you do this, it will help because you will not have a credit history established in the United States when you arrive and you may otherwise have trouble getting a card here. Credit cards charge interest on the balance (the money you owe), and the interest is often very high. Try to keep little or no balance on your cards. Be very careful with your credit card and protect your number. Check your statements and keep track of your receipts. Shred or destroy any document that has your card number on it or even the offer of a new credit card. Credit card theft is common, and a thief can destroy your credit history if you do not notify the credit card company of theft in a timely manner. If you see unusual purchase activity or purchases you did not make on your credit card statement, report that to the credit card company immediately; your statement includes a telephone number for reporting "fraud."

Telephone Service

When you move into your dormitory room, apartment, or house, you will want to establish telephone service. There are a variety of local and long-distance service options, including reduced rates for international calls. Be careful about making too many international calls; even with the best rates, it can get expensive. It is not unusual to hear that some students' monthly telephone bills are $200 to $300 or higher. Get as much information about each service option, and choose the best one to fit your needs. It is also possible to purchase long-distance calling cards that can be used like an ongoing account. Be careful to shop for the best deals.

Cell Phones

Very popular and prevalent in the United States, cell phones are increasingly replacing traditional "land lines." They can be useful and convenient; however, they are not to be considered necessary or required. Cell phones and the payment plans that go with them can be expensive, and you can be bound to contracts as long as two years. Some cell phone plans are better than others, so shop wisely and read the terms carefully. A good plan will give you plenty of minutes to use your phone each month without additional charges, free long distance, and no hidden roaming charges. Roaming charges are fees that some providers charge when you use your phone outside of your service area. A good plan also allows you to have unlimited in-network calls. If you have friends or relatives in the United States that you will need to communicate with on a regular basis, ask them who their service provider is. By getting the same service, you could save money.

Internet Service and Email Service

Email is widely accessible, and most colleges and universities give their students email and on-campus access to the Internet. Colleges and universities value the richness offered by the Internet, and many courses have online content and activities that are required. In addition, colleges and universities often subscribe to many research databases and online journals. Make sure to become aware of the online resources available to you. The school library is generally a good place to begin.

You will have to consider Internet service for your off-campus housing or dorm room if it is not provided by the college. The cost of Internet service can vary with the dial-up as low as $9 a month, and high-speed cable access costing up to $60. As with cell phones, shop carefully and be sure to fully understand the terms of your service. Some providers offer low introductory fees to lure you into their service and then raise the price significantly after a few months.

Many businesses and colleges provide wireless access to the Internet. Take full advantage of wireless access and its convenience. The $40–$80 cost for a "wireless" card for a laptop is a good investment.

As a student, having your own access to the Internet is a beneficial resource if used properly. Not only can it help with your studies, it can also keep phone bills down if you can communicate with your family, relatives, and friends back home via email. It is becoming easier to use the Internet to communicate in real time, much like using a telephone. This is an inexpensive option that is dependent on how sophisticated the Internet is in your home country.

More Internet-related issues will be discussed in Chapters 7 and 11.

Getting Ready for the First Day of Classes

You have finally settled into your new living space and have registered, confirmed your registration, and paid for your classes. You are ready to begin, and it is probably several days away from the first day of class. There are many issues that you could take care of while you are waiting.

First, become more familiar with the school. Find out as much as you can about the services provided. Find out about recreational facilities, sports programs, social events, clubs, and transportation. Also try to go off campus and find out what the surrounding area has to offer.

Another thing that you could do is to buy your textbooks. Do not forget to keep your receipt! Sometimes classes are cancelled, the professor may change the books, or you may need to change classes. Also, do not write in your books until you are firmly in the class. You may not want to write in your books at all because many schools and bookstores will buy back your textbooks for resale. In addition, you may want to cut down on the amount you pay for textbooks by buying those marked "used."

Check the local area and see if there are other bookstores that support your school. You might also check some online booksellers and compare their prices, including shipping costs, with the campus bookstore. If you buy your texts online, make sure you understand their return policies. As indicated, things can change, and you do not want to be stuck with expensive books that you don't need.

The First Day!

The first day of classes can be both very interesting and very confusing. It is a challenging day for everyone, so if you experience uncertainty or anxiousness, then you are having normal feelings. A word of advice: Be on time to class! Punctuality is important for most professors (even if they are sometimes not punctual themselves).

Patience is important on the first day. Be prepared for the possibility that what you presumed would be an orderly movement through the day may seem more like chaos. Colleges and universities are like any other large institutions, and sometimes small changes have great results. Classes can get moved from one room to another, or even cancelled; information about such changes is often just a note on the door. If you cannot find a class or if one of your classes is cancelled, see your ISA or an academic counselor for help. If a class is cancelled and brings your course load down to less than full-time, you must find a new class to replace it. We have mentioned this already: It is your responsibility to maintain a full-time load of classes.

Your first day of each class will most likely consist of an introductory session and the distribution of the course syllabus (description and list of assignments). The professor might give a verbal description of the course and the objectives and present what he or she expects from the students. If a professor does not do this, then the information is usually written in the syllabus. If expectations are not clear to you, ask questions or arrange to see your professor during his or her office hours.

Do not expect your class or your professor to be like classes and professors in your own country. They may be very different and the professors may expect things of you that are different from what you anticipate (see Chapter 5 for a detailed analysis).

CHAPTER 4

Overcoming Stress

I t is said that when visiting a town nearby, Nasraddin Hodja, a character in Turkish fairy tales, was stopped by a man who asked what day of the week it was. "I cannot tell you," Nasraddin Hodja replied to the man. "I am a stranger in this town. I do not know what day of the week they have here." This anecdote suggests that we sometimes see the differences between America and our home country as greater than they really are. For some people, their personal difficulties, inability to communicate well in a new language, and lower than expected achievement are easy to explain by differences between cultures. "This country is so different from mine that I cannot be successful here," some may think. Psychologists say that the process of adjustment to a new culture is not easy. Your first steps are often accompanied by an **acculturated stress,** an initial reaction of adjustment to a different cultural environment. This type of stress has many different forms and is felt by individuals in a variety of ways. But in most situations, it is an unpleasant experience. This chapter examines what various people say about their initial adjustment to the United States. We will later discuss what students can do to overcome their stress.

Stress as Nostalgia

For many who come to a foreign country, stress is a reaction of sadness about missing something very dear to our heart. We leave our friends and relatives. We often miss food, familiar smells, colors, and landscapes. Here are just a few examples taken from student interviews:

- "At the beginning, I missed the food. My childhood was built on that." (J. J., Afghanistan)

- "I definitely was missing the town, the mountains, and the Caspian Sea." (A. A., Iran)

- "I missed the smell of my home country, the early morning smell. You have to experience this to understand me." (R. D., India)

- "Trees, definitely the trees, and the aroma of hay. And the snow. I was missing it, too." (K. R., Russia)

Nostalgia is a bittersweet longing for things and situations of the past, especially those that are impossible to get back to. Sometimes nostalgia is associated with people.

- "I missed my big family. I felt empty without it. It was a devastating [feeling] during my first year here." (K. O., Bolivia)

- "I lost the connection. People in my country have closer ties with each other than people here have. I missed open doors that we had at home." (T. T., Russia)

- "I missed family gatherings, holidays, family prayer, and dancing together. Now I can deal with this. But at the beginning, my sadness was huge." (M. K., Ethiopia).

- "Above everything else, I missed my friends. I clearly remember this feeling of sadness." (R. K., Korea).

> # Think Critically
>
> Have you experienced these feelings of loss? Do you experience them now? If you can, please share with others about who and what you miss the most from your home country. Or write in a journal about what you miss. What do you do about these unpleasant feelings?

Our anxiety and nostalgia are often based on feelings of separation:

- "I have never been isolated from my family before. That year was my first time alone, and it contributed to my painful experiences. I missed my parents, my family. I was blaming America for my misery when, in fact, it was just a discomfort caused by my separation," said a 22-year-old student from Venezuela describing her emotional stress. (A. L., Venezuela)

Stress as Loss of Personal Control

Some people may lose some sense of control of the events around them. Simple things—such as knowing a weather forecast for the next day, finding local news, and being able to buy a certain food—may sometimes bring a sense of comfort. Unfortunately, especially during the first weeks and months of adjustment, these small things are missing for many of those who are new to this country. This loss of personal control can create anxiety and frustration. Why does it happen?

In our home countries, we rely on our friends, important customs, and even unspoken rules that connect people. In most situations, we knew what to say and how to act. America is different from our homes, and it takes time to learn the new rules, to make new friends, and to acquire new habits. "Back home, I used to solve all my problems by picking up the phone," an engineer from Turkey recalls his first college year in America. "When I moved [to the United States], it was especially difficult to accept the fact that my old connections meant nothing here." But before we learn the new rules, there is confusion that may last quite a long time. "First of all, I didn't have friends," said Mary, a 24-year-old student from South Africa. "I had no idea what people my age were into. I didn't know if the movies or mall were the cool places to hang out. I didn't even know what people of my age were like. I felt like I was being pulled in many different ways. Should I be changed just to meet the American lifestyle? Should I stay where I was? I was confused."

> ## Think Critically
>
> Did you experience a loss of personal control over the events around you after your arrival to the United States? If yes, how long did it last? Who did you expect to help you? Who helped you the most during your first month in the United States?

Do not forget that the more control you have over events around you, the more comfortable you feel, and the less noticeable the stress.

Stress as Dissatisfaction with Language Barriers

For many people, stress is associated with an unpleasant experience of misunderstanding and isolation. Language problems significantly reduce the number of people you are able to have contact with. Dissatisfaction with the new life, therefore, can become overwhelming. One 19-year-old Ukrainian student recalled her first day in America: "I was left alone in a foreign country, knowing nobody, speaking no language, having no idea of what was going on. I couldn't read the street signs, and I felt myself like on another planet." Isolation may have multiple consequences. The same student continued: "Even being here for about a year, because of my [poor] language, I am still afraid to meet people, the 'real' Americans."

This is how another young woman describes her first-year experiences in America after her family moved here from Thailand: "I didn't understand people around me. I hated school and everybody in it. I couldn't wait to go home where I felt safe and secure. Everyone had someone to talk and walk with during lunch. I was always by myself about everywhere I went. I felt so hurt that I cried when no one was around."

"Since my English skills were poor, I tended to trust whatever people told me," reported a 29-year-old student from Philippines. "I tried to convince myself that my skills were not bad, but I kept making so many bad judgments based on my poor language skills. I was not only losing money and comfort, I was losing my self-confidence. I could speak the language well enough to get around, but I wasn't proficient. And the saddest thing for me was my inability to understand jokes. That is why many newcomers do not feel very comfortable in America during first several months because they do not get all those sarcastic and other funny things, especially on TV."

A personal sense of isolation is a major challenge, and there are not many effective ways to fight it alone. Until adequate communication skills are achieved, many people withdraw, while others remain frustrated for a long time.

Think Critically

Have you experienced misunderstandings with other people? Have you ever felt embarrassed because of this? Did you feel that sometimes people could not understand you? Did you feel disappointed about having these problems? Did you ever blame yourself for the lack of your language skills?

Stress as Loss of Habits and Lifestyle

Stress may be reflected by a change of the individual's lifestyle. Like being in a dark room with no lights on, you have to examine every unfamiliar object just to get around: The time you wake up and go to bed, the breakfast you have, the newspapers you read, the people you call, the friends you meet, the food you buy, and the problems you solve. Everything is rearranged like pieces in a jigsaw puzzle. "Suddenly we were told that we would be moving to America," recalls a business major from Peru. "I remember I took a look at our tiny apartment because my dad said that I might never see it again. I didn't believe him, but he was right. Everything changes so suddenly. From being a child and a follower, I have changed and become a serious man. Within a month, I have changed because here in America I didn't have that laid-back atmosphere that we had back home."

Perhaps the most difficult thing is not all the rules and customs of the United States, but the need to follow these practices and customs. "I hated everything here during my first months. I realized that the rules of behavior here were stricter than those in Argentina," noted a 24-year-old business major. "People obey the rules here. I remember my impressions about traffic in Portland. Cars are standing in lanes and follow each other. In Argentina, you use any and every shortcut to get there faster: any pavement, an opposite side

Think Critically

Loss of habits or lifestyle is not necessarily an unpleasant experience. One of our students suggested that right after he became a student, he developed many valuable skills that helped him to be independent. Now think about yourself. After your arrival to the United States, did you acquire new habits that you consider useful and valuable? Have you lost any habits that you're glad not to have?

of the road, you run a red light. I know some people do it here, but it is uncommon. I may sound like I am a bad person, but I am saying how difficult it was to change my habits."

One Korean student recalls how she was brought to the United States at age 11 and was moved to a small rural town in the Midwest. Being "normal" and "regular" in Korea, she suddenly became the center of attention in the town. The family found itself in a spotlight. It was a friendly attitude, both curious and sympathetic. "We were the only Asian family in town. People would turn around to stare at us. We were different from the local crowd," she told me with a smile. "Did you have cows in Korea? Do people use flush toilets? Do people sing songs in Korea?" These and many other questions of this kind were addressed to her family every day. She reported that the change from being "almost invisible" in her home country to being a local celebrity was overwhelming. The family found itself in a human zoo, on constant display.

Stress as Perceived Differences

We do not live in vacuums. We must continuously adjust to the new. Discovery is usually a pleasant experience. However, there is a difference between discovering something new and accepting it. We have seen many cases when a person would experience stress because of his or her strong desire to conform to mainstream norms but then was unable to do so. An example of this is the difficulty some students have in maintaining their religious practices in the context of their class and study schedules. More campuses are now aware of this and are providing convenient space for meditation and prayer. On the other hand, some individuals are able to protect themselves from stress because they do not conform at all, instead preserving surroundings typical of their home country. These individuals only speak the native language, only communicate with people from the same ethnic group, and try not to travel outside of their neighborhood. However, living in such an isolated environment is impossible for the student. We have to be able to live in the world of values and norms that are different from those of our cultures.

We are all used to doing certain things in a particular way, like praying, celebrating holidays, following customs, singing, eating, and speaking. We experience difficulties when the current situation requires us to follow the majority that does these things differently or doesn't do them at all. One student living in Virginia recalled his early experiences with America: "Food was a surprise to me. Koreans eat kimchi, a traditional food with garlic and pepper. It gives you a garlic breath. I realized how people here disliked this odor. I stopped eating it after several weeks here and that was very difficult to me because American traditional food was tasteless for me at that time. Another tradition was also difficult to follow: Americans wear shoes in the house, but Koreans never do that. First, I felt extremely embarrassed when people didn't let me take off my shoes when I was visiting their homes, and I felt that others were rude when they didn't take off their shoes in my home."

Obviously, similarities between your home culture and American life may substantially reduce your stress.

Think
Critically

Some vivid differences between American culture and other cultures are mentioned frequently in the interviews (1995–2007) collected by Shiraev and Levy (2007). *Question:* Do you agree with these observations listed below? Do you think that some people exaggerate the differences between America and their home countries? What can you add to or delete from this list?

- The clothes that some people wear in the United States are considered "strange," "shocking," and "revealing" (reported primarily by students who grew up in small towns or rural areas).
- People on the street do not pay attention to you (reported primarily by those who live and study in big metropolitan areas).
- Food is tasteless or not spicy enough (reported generally about fast food).
- Traffic on the roads is overwhelming (reported primarily by those who live in big metropolitan areas).
- Toilets are unusually clean and free of charge (reported primarily by students from both rural areas and from developing countries).
- Television is shocking and revealing (reported primarily by people from traditional cultures).
- Telephones and emails are overused—i.e., everything is solved over the phone or online. There is little personal contact among people (reported primarily by people from traditional countries).
- Young people are not cultured, and many are not really respectful to adults (reported by most observers).

Stress as Perceived Value Differences

How often did you feel that your personal values were different from the values of most people around you? How often do you notice that people can freely and carelessly talk about something like sex or other intimate issues that you consider shameful? How often do you notice that everybody avoids talking about something that you feel is indeed simple and understandable? Many values that may have been accepted in your culture are not understood or even respected in the host country. One of the elements of stress is disappointment based on perceived differences of values between two cultures. Which values that are widely accepted in the United States are sometimes difficult to accept by those who are going through an adjustment process? Some common themes regarding value differences follow.

American Pragmatism

Values associated with material success and achievement are seen not only as typical American traits, but are things that disappoint and cause resentment by many individuals during their initial stage of adjustment. To many people in America, pragmatism is a key to professional and personal success, yet some others fail, at least initially. This causes frustration. "Pragmatism is shown everywhere. There is little spontaneity in life. Everything is calculated. You have to make an appointment to take somebody for lunch," noted a 26-year-old Russian student of her impressions during the first year.

American pragmatism is often seen as instant categorization of everything, as a student from El Salvador complained to us: "I was really surprised at the beginning with how here in America things should be categorized. Everything should be on its shelf! Sports teams receive ranks. Music groups have ranks. The stock market is all about numbers. Opinion polls are [published] in every newspaper, and people also have to be put in racial categories, for example, when they fill out a government form."

Disappointment with American pragmatism may be also explained by the fact that most people who try to settle in the United States are neither rich nor well-to-do individuals. Most newcomers work hard for their money to pay bills, and wonder why so many people around them care about investment, whereas many new comers cannot maintain even a minimum balance in their checking account. Indeed, many Americans inherited substantial wealth from their parents and ancestors. The top 1 percent of households owned about 33 percent of all privately held wealth in the early 2000s (Kessler 2005). And millions of individuals born and raised in this country over the past 200-plus years have been able to save more money and establish more connections than millions of those who are still relatively new to this country. Disappointment with materialism causes frustration in some people because they hoped to have immediate benefits of their effort but, for various reasons, could not. This frustration may cause rejection of the existing reality and prolong one's stress.

Think Critically

Do you agree with this description of American pragmatism given to us from a student from Spain?

"People here are self-absorbed and stressed. The pressure of life and work in this area seem to take its toll on the quality of life. People have conceivable material comfort and high-tech equipment, and yet many are not happy. People do not even find the time to enjoy a sunset. In comparison, although the pace and pressure of life in Madrid is also intense, it is more a group-oriented, cafe-style society, where social interaction and verbal communications are their 'daily bread'! The American lives to work; in Spain, they work to live."

Do you think that it is possible to interpret American pragmatism from a different, more positive, perspective? Could you suggest, for example, that American people work hard and enjoy working? Could you imply that every nation has its own style of work and leisure and that Americans are not necessarily unhappy because they have such busy lives? Why or why not?

American Individualism

Individualism is a concern for oneself and one's immediate family as opposed to collectivism, a concern for the larger social groups to which one belongs. In the individualistic culture, people are independent both vertically (people of both higher and lower status levels) and horizontally (people of the same status level). In collectivist cultures, group goals (related to country, community, work, religion, education, and cultural traditions) play the most important role in the individual's life. In individualistic cultures, the goals of the individual and his or her immediate family are the most important ones. Every culture has elements of collectivism and individualism. However, America is viewed by a vast majority of people as a culture with predominantly individualistic features. For many people, especially for those who grew up in collectivist societies, America is seen as a relatively cold, indifferent country filled with selfish individuals. This is, of course, an inaccurate perception.

Think
Critically

Do you think that American individualism is necessarily a negative characteristic of people and society in general? Do you think that such issues as respect for private property, individual privacy, and civil freedoms can be considered as aspects of American individualism? Please find and discuss examples of positive impact of individualism on people's lives. Find examples of American collectivism.

Such contrasts of experience sharpen negative evaluations of present conditions and contribute to stress. "People have so many opportunities to do things on their own that they do not value friendship," suggested one 19-year-old student from Morocco after spending three years in Ohio. Very often, perceived differences in norms convince people that Americans are noncaring. "The families in the U.S. are not nearly as close-knit as those in West Africa. There almost everyone just stays with their families for their whole lives. There was open space for children and animals to run and play together. It was my biggest challenge here to get used to empty streets and empty front yards," points out a 24-year-old nurse. "People are superficially friendly here," said a 20-year-old student from Honduras. "It was deceiving at the beginning of my life here and therefore my disappointment was especially strong. People ask questions and do not care about your answers. You ask a person 'how are you' and he will reply 'fine' without even looking at you."

Americans Have "Too Much" Freedom

When the words *too much* are used, the question can be asked, "too much, compared to what?" It is common for many of us to long for the good times when things seemed to be more certain, the grass greener, the skies bluer, and everything appeared to be in its place. From another standpoint, "too much freedom" would probably mean that today people are granted opportunities and allowed to exercise behaviors that were not considered appropriate some time ago. For the newcomers, however, the expression "too much freedom" is associated with their own perceptions of freedom formed in their home countries. Those perceptions, of course, have been shaped according to particular religious principles, ethnic customs, cultural norms, and even political traditions. For a Dutch businessman, American culture could be seen as more restrictive, compared to his home country, where, for example, marijuana and prostitution are conditionally legalized. A student from Greece or Russia would notice how much stricter the anti-smoking rules are in the United States than in their countries. However, for millions of people coming to the United States, this country's norms are seen as more "loose" than the norms of their home countries. "My biggest source of stress was the realization that here people have too much freedom. There is no code. Some men wear long hair; [some] women shave their heads. That was both amazing and disturbing," recalls a student from a southern Indian province.

Think
Critically

Very often, public misperceptions feed people's expectations about America and produce unreasonable expectations and wrong opinions. For example, there have been several highly publicized cases about American children challenging their parents in courts. Americans have expressed a wide range of diversified opinions about these cases. However, around the world, the cases in which children filed suit against their parents were frequently portrayed in the media as "typical American." What one 18-year-old student, born in Pakistan, recalled about his initial perception of America five years ago is interesting. "My father had told me that we are moving to a country where children can sue their parents. He wasn't joking. He was serious. I saw his eyes when he explained it to our mother. And they both shook their heads. I was scared first because I felt that everyone would sue me here. I didn't completely understand the meaning of this word, but I knew it was something really bad, when a child can put his parents in jail."

Question: Can you recall any incorrect perceptions or expectations you had about the United States prior to your arrival here that later changed once you arrived or where your opinions changed to be more positive?

Having too much freedom or too many options to choose from is not always associated with anxiety and distress. For some individuals, this experience may become stimulating and rewarding. "Moving from the British-African system of education to the United States was quite a surprise. We went from being slapped by a teacher for having your hands in your pockets, to the environment where people do not seem to care what you wear to school. In Zim (our abbreviation for Zimbabwe), we were required to spend at least five hours of homework each weekend," said K. K., a 21-year-old, student.

"What I was surprised [about] the most was freedom of speech in classes," suggested a 35-year-old college professor, born in Egypt, who completed his education in New York. "I sometimes felt embarrassed to hear the students' questions and comments, sometimes about intimate topics, but mostly about the government. Students called professors by their first names and, in many other occasions, some students showed disrespect to their teachers. And that was almost a norm. I felt very uncomfortable during my first year as a student."

For others, the existing freedoms cause an entirely different psychological experience, as in this man from Bangladesh: "My shock was obvious. Coming from a highly regimented culture, I was overwhelmed with freedom that literally crushed on my shoulders. I didn't know what to do with it. One of the most amazing and difficult things was overcoming problems to choose; there were many available options here in America."

Think
Critically

Sometimes, stress can be a motivational, positive experience. Here is an excerpt from an interview from M. R., 25, born in Greece. "My first year in Los Angeles was like a football match to me, when your team is winning. Everything was great. I was excited since I planned my arrival here for a long period of time. I was finally free, and my head full of plans and projects. Everybody was helpful to me. During the first year, I learned a lot, everything was interesting, and I kept staring at many things with my eyes wide open."

Question: What was your most pleasant experience during the first three months in the United States?

After having read the chapter thus far, could you describe what acculturative stress is? Is it a personal problem or personal growth? Is it a learning experience or loss of control over life events? Indeed, for some individuals, their initial stages of adjustment are remembered as the most exciting period of their lives, but for others it was interpreted as a fearful journey into the unknown. For some people, stress is an anticipated relief, but for many others it is a road with thousands of abrupt curves and obstacles. For some, stress is nothing but pain and grief. For others, it is just a stressful period of learning. The problem of the existing explanations of stress is that, in fact, different types of stress were described by different individuals who were going through different stages of their stress and were affected by different social and psychological conditions. For example, stress experienced by a refugee from Sudan, a mother of two, might be totally different from the stress experienced by a Brazilian or German exchange student.

It is true that understanding a problem alone may not change a problem. Understanding is a first step toward practical solutions to help overcome stress if it occurs. Let us examine some of the existing ways to effectively adjust to a new cultural environment. Do not forget that there is no single and universal procedure for culture-shock reduction. Every person chooses his or her own way.

Managing the Stress

Change Your Thinking

An Irish proverb says that if God shuts one door, He opens another. Wouldn't it be nice to discover these open doors for all people? For many of us, it seems we face only those doors that have been shut. This is the problem. Psychologists suggest that not the events around us, but also our pessimistic thinking about the events (when one sees only the shut doors, for example) causes psychological problems. Events in themselves do not cause negative emotions. Instead, unhappiness and anxiety are mainly due to our pessimistic description of events (Ellis 1962). From this standpoint, stress can be interpreted as a result of a person's negative thinking.

Consider this example: Albert G., a 22-year-old exchange student, arrived in the United States six months ago. From the beginning of his life here, he has been experiencing symptoms of disappointment and persistent anxiety. He was also overwhelmed with pessimistic thoughts. According to the approach we are using now, Albert's symptoms should not be interpreted as negative developments caused by his arrival to a new country. The fact that stress follows migration doesn't prove that migration is the cause of stress. (Likewise, the winter doesn't cause the spring just because the spring follows the winter!) Therefore, we should try to give a different interpretation of the causes of Albert's stress.

For instance, as Albert explained to us, he was always a disciplined boy and young man who liked to plan everything in his life and tried to achieve perfection in every endeavor. Moving to the United States caused a disruption in his lifestyle when he temporarily became unable to control things and events around him. At the same time, Albert's habitual desire to be successful and even perfect caused his emotional displeasure: His grades at school were not as good as he wanted them to be. In his home country, he was able to achieve some important goals, and his college grades were perfect. In the new culture, his old patterns of thinking no longer worked for him. It was not going to be possible for him to be perfect from the start in the United States. What should he do?

Under these circumstances, Albert should change his self-perception of himself as a "successful individual within a perfectly organized environment" and accept a different view of life. This means that for the time of his initial adjustment, which may last for several months, he should accept a view that would suspend his previously held perceptions on his own success. All in all, he doesn't have to be perfect, successful, and mistake-free during the period of adjustment!

Sergei Tsytsarev, a psychotherapist from Hofstra University, has told us that those newcomers who view their present life situation including their stress in a more positive way adjust better than those who view their life in predominantly negative terms (Tsytsarev and Grodnitsky 1995). Moreover, studies show that people who are aware of their own feelings can exert greater control over their reactions to events (Perls 1973). Yes, it is possible to encourage an individual to take responsibility for his or her actions rather than blame other people or even the entire society for misery and suffering they could bring. As one Chinese proverb suggests, two-thirds of that we see is behind our eyes. Therefore, it is almost imperative to look around frequently. Sometimes we have to do this more often than we currently do.

Accept the Reality around You

Other specialists believe that our psychological problems during stress are caused by our inability to address the changes that we cannot control. We all gain and lose things; we all go through easy and difficult periods of life, and we have to accept anything that happens. For many people, stress is in part a nostalgic reaction of a loss—the loss of homeland, relatives, and familiar places. Therefore, for those who experience stress, the loss should be articulated, explained. In a simple way, this should be one's rational understanding, agreement with, and acceptance of the fact of the loss: This is my life, and it should be accepted as it is. You cannot step twice into the same river, pointed out the Greek philosopher Heraclitus. This remarkable idea was shared with us during one interview with a 30-year-old woman from Peru: "I only now realized that many of my unpleasant feelings of loss associated with Peru are, in fact, my sadness about [losing] my happy childhood. Once I was a girl and it was when I lived in Peru. I will never become a child again. And all my happy recollections about my innocent life of a little girl are associated with my home country. Now I have learned to enjoy my age and understand that I will never become small again."

"The lowest ebb is the turn of the tide," wrote Henry Longfellow, an American poet, more than 100 years ago. Accepting this wisdom and applying it to one's life may indeed become an inspiration. Self-encouragement may also exist in some people in the form of a specific plan in life. As a young man from India told us, "I overcame my stress because I knew what to do with my life: I had a goal to become a doctor." Others form a general attitude of being busy, as one interviewee said about her mother: "By deliberately keeping herself busy with her everyday work, she forgot the fact that she was alone in a faraway land." It is important to know, nevertheless, that self-encouragement may become ineffective, especially if you do not have enough time or resources to overcome the problems that you face. Unrealistic expectations may cause significant problems in initial adjustment.

Acquire a New Attitude

"In the hour of adversity be not without hope, for crystal rain falls from black clouds," wrote Nizami, a great Persian poet. A recovery from stress can begin with self-evaluation, followed by adopting a healthier attitude. Look around you, and find those areas in which you feel your weakness. Let your weakness become your strength. How can you achieve this? By changing the way you think about yourself. For example, what if some people do not understand your English? You have time: Self-improvement will follow, and very soon everyone will realize that you speak two languages fluently (both your native tongue and English), whereas most people around you speak only one! Do some people think of you as a helpless foreigner? Again, in time you will be able to prove that you can become as successful as others. "I felt from the beginning I had to do twice as much as others were doing to prove myself as worthy as an American person," said a businessman from Iran, describing how he felt when he was brought to the United States as a teenager. "I said to myself, you have to be twice as better as people around you, especially if you are a minority person," recalled one student from Liberia, commenting on his recovery from pessimistic thinking and fears that were haunting him for months after his arrival to these shores. It is unfair, of course, to do twice as much as others do in order to succeed. But while it takes years and even centuries to change an unfair social system, it may take significantly less time to change one's attitude on the personal level. Remember, self-encouragement is a source of inspiration.

Developing a healthy attitude is often a process of reevaluating expectations. Unrealistic hopes can cause poor adjustment and prolong stress. "Many newcomers have to adjust their expectations. Many of us have false perceptions of what life is like in America. We watch films and read magazines, and when we come here we realize that it is less idyllic than we thought it would be. "Life in America is not the *Baywatch* adventures or an *Independence Day* fairy tale," a student from Greece explained. A student's expectations may seem reasonable at first. For example, a young woman from Nigeria anticipated that she would do fine in the United States because of her command of the English language, spoken since birth. However, she was shocked to realize that people in a small Michigan town could hardly understand her because of her specific accent, even though she spoke grammatically correct English. The shock and disappointment were frustrating and added to her stress.

Accepting a new attitude or reevaluating one's expectations won't happen overnight. But even these relatively lengthy processes may be accelerated. Take one step at a time. Do not rush; be patient. Instead of trying to solve everything at once, decide what is the most urgent problem for you, and concentrate on that first. Here is how one Iranian man described his strategy during his first college year: "At the beginning when I came here, I was trying to solve my immediate problems. I didn't have any long-lasting problems that other people have because I tried to focus on my immediate things. My life was like a military operation: you do this; you solve that. I always tried to calculate my next step."

Perhaps you will set high goals and ambitions, but remember to be realistic. Make one decision today, not two decisions, because the second one can be made tomorrow. Expect small successes and incremental achievements. Do not look at others who seem to be doing better than you are. Everyone is different. Choose your own pace of moving ahead. As German poet Wolfgang von Goethe wrote almost 200 years ago, "What each day needs, that shalt you ask, each day will set its proper task." We think his poetic advice sounds just right for modern times.

Make Things More Familiar to You

"All problems become smaller if you do not dodge them," said renowned American naval officer, William Halsey. To articulate one's problem and adjust one's attitude are the first steps of problem solving. Do not *wait* for things to become familiar.

According to a Turkish fairy tale, a neighbor came up to Nasraddin Hodja (the popular hero of Turkish fairy tales whose remarks opened this chapter) and complained that there was no sunlight in his house. "Is there any sunlight in your garden?" Hodja asked. "Yes, certainly," replied the man. "Then move your house into your garden," suggested Hodja.

Of course one cannot bring his or her home, friends, and relatives to the United States and put them in a house on the same street. On the other hand, you can bring something from your home culture, and you can learn what most Americans do. "You know how we took care of our holidays in America? We celebrated both Muslim and Christian holidays. Christmas? Easter? No problem," said a student who came here from Iran in the early 1990s. "We cel-

✎ A Class Assignment

I placed a blank piece of paper before a student and said, "I've told you about the stress that many people experience when they arrive in a new country. Now write everything that bothers you in your present situation." I offered him a pen. "In each sentence," I continued, "describe the things that you want to have and the obstacles that prevent you from getting these things done."

It took him a little time before he began to write with a smile. "I want to bring my family here, but (he hesitated for a second) I cannot do it at this time," he looked at me.

I nodded in response. "Fine, continue, please."

"I do not like this weather, but my education is the reason why I stay here. I would like to have many friends, but I dislike some people around me. I need somebody to talk with about my personal things, but I always have to speak English; I cannot express myself well in English." There were more things written on that page.

"Now listen to this," I said and gave him a red pen. "Take a look at the list and substitute each use of *but* with *and*. Just erase every *but* and insert *and*. So what do you have now?" After a minute, he started reading:

> *I want to bring my family here and I cannot do it at this time. I do not like this weather and my education is the reason why I stay here. I would like to have many friends and I dislike many people around me. I need somebody to talk with about some personal things and I always have to speak English; I cannot express myself in English.*

I continued: "You see, by making these simple substitutions, you just corrected the way you see some problems. Now you may see your problems not as dilemmas, but as things that coexist with other things! These different aspects do not seem like contradictions any longer and then you learn how to live with them . . . "

"I understand," he replied after reading the sentences again. "This looks nice on a piece of paper, but how can I act this way?"

"Yes, it's difficult. But—" I smiled," *and*—let me correct myself too because I cannot use *but*—it's a long way and you have to begin with small things. Just remember this list and repeat it to yourself once a day. Begin with a change in your mind."

Assignment: Repeat the procedure described in this case. Please write four or five problems that bother, upset, frustrate you today. In each sentence, put a desirable outcome first, then write *but* and describe what prevents you from getting what you want to have or do. After you finish the sentences, erase every *but* and insert instead *and*. Now can you see your problems differently? Discuss your notes in class.

ebrate our [Muslim] religious holidays as religious events, and consider local [Christian] holidays as the time for fun, guests, and gifts."

Psychologists call creating your own psychological environment the *self-discovery method*. Here the individual creates his or her own social climate in which he or she feels comfortable. Observing and celebrating traditional holidays, commemorating great leaders of your country, or organizing special events and parties may stimulate promotion of self-acceptance. Self-discovery should not lead to self-isolation, as sometimes happens. For example, we knew a person from England who could not manage to settle into American life. She felt desperately homesick and could not function in America, constantly complaining about culture differences between England and the United States.

The similarities and differences we find around us are based on our descriptions. Descriptions, in turn, are always made from a particular point of view. Try to change your point of view, and you will see things differently. A change in the perception could lead to a more pleasant feeling. "I think that for people who came here from Iran just before the revolution, their stress wasn't so difficult to overcome. Despite many differences, these two cultures had many things in common," said a professional who was brought here as a teenager right after the Iranian Shah gave up power. "After you told me about the similarities, I began to discover that people in my country act in almost the same way that the people in America," suggested a student from South Africa.

Some may even compare their experiences back home to their experiences here, always trying to find a positive side in the new experiences. One example of such comparison follows.

- It was warmer in Iraq, but here I spend most of my time at home, in the office, or in the car. I do not feel the cold in the winter.
- The food was spicier at home, but here I also can go to our ethnic restaurants and eat my favorite dishes; besides I can cook at home.
- Most of my friends and relatives are in El Salvador; but here I also have many friends, and I even find sometimes that there are more of them than I would like to have.

Psychologists have suggested for a long time that, like our old models of thinking, our old problem-solving strategies do not necessarily work in new environments. When you are "prompted to behave in the new setting using back-home cues, you will most likely to encounter trouble" (Brislin and Pedersen 1976). Elizabeth Goldston, a professional translator, reminded us about the tale of Gulliver, a man who was cast adrift in open seas and finally came ashore in the Land of the Houyhnhnms. There he encountered a new and strange culture wherein his initial assumptions, based on his previous cultural experience, proved completely inaccurate. Like Gulliver, in the process of resettling elsewhere we may find that all our previously acquired cultural knowledge becomes a poor compass to guide us through the quicksand of unfamiliar mores and customs of the new society. This assumption does not mean that we shouldn't use our old models of behavior. The point is that we ought to use them critically. We may have to compromise, but finding a middle course is not always about giving up something. Rather, it is adding to our new conditions an environment in which you feel comfortable and can perform effectively. Some critics say that by doing this we keep one foot on one bank of the river while trying to reach the other bank with the other foot. We would say, "We are not trying to step over the river. We are building a bridge."

Learn from Others

You do not need to wait for others to teach you. One approach psychologists use is called *participant modeling*. It requires an individual to acquire social skills by performing adaptive behaviors. To manage stress effectively, you have to learn the behaviors that are healthy and useful for you today and get rid of those that are not useful. Using this approach, it would be inaccurate to suggest that "people who are pessimistic expect the worst." Instead, it would be more accurate to say that "people who expect the worst are pessimistic." Likewise, it is incorrect to say that people with stress experience anxiety based on their disappointment with the United States. Instead, we would say that those newcomers who are disappointed with their lives here are experiencing continuous stress.

This method of thinking must be learned and applied to new experiences to achieve new behavior. There are other methods that can be adopted for stress management. Most of these methods assume a similar foundation: psychological training, which produces not only greater knowledge but develops new adaptive skills in participating individuals. Training methods accelerate the process of adaptation and make your behavior more productive. "They chew a ton of wood for an ounce of honey," says a Turkish proverb about those who do not have such behavioral skills. (It shows how not having training to accelerate adaptation is more work.) There is wisdom in old proverbs.

Another helpful technique is to surround yourself with people during your initial adjustment. Provide yourself with a wide range of role models. Find encouragement from others with similar problems who can provide you with assurance that your problems are not unique and give you the opportunity to try out a new behavior. "When I got my first job, my manager, who also had come to America just five years ago, helped me a lot. She began to push me to do particular things, to overcome fears that I thought were impossible to defeat. I started to change, I could feel it," recalls a student from Afghanistan.

This *social-relations technique* could be used on a college campus or in a similar setting where there is a wide selection of individuals with the same type of problems. A discussion on stress where people can meet each other, share their concerns, and learn that others have similar problems, could be helpful. A facilitator of such a meeting should be someone who has already overcome stress and is able to share his or her experiences. It may be desirable to hold such meetings on a regular basis. It is not always necessary, however, to keep ethnic similarity of such groups. Finding other people with whom you may have some common interests could reduce feelings of isolation.

Another successful method is *social skills training* in which people rehearse new behavior in group settings. The difference here is that the focus is mainly on learning specific skills and behavioral responses. Such tasks as making a phone call, purchasing a car, or filling out an application may be successfully rehearsed with other people in role-playing situations. In real life, we learn how to do these things alone or with the help of our friends. We learn from both our own mistakes and from the experience of others. In a training situation, we also gain experience and learn from mistakes, but we do it in specially designed settings where mistakes will be immediately corrected.

This method could be very helpful in learning the language or improving conversational skills. For instance, you can learn a set of phrases that are adaptive in particular situations. You can learn how to say no without being disrespectful, how to make a request, or how to place a phone call. Such learned phrases help build confidence and allow you to be more relaxed. In one of our workshops, for example, newly arrived students learned with joy how to be part of a standard greeting exchange between two Americans. If you are asked: *Hi, how are you?* Simply answer: *Thanks, I am fine. How about yourself?* And then when you hear: *Just fine, thanks,* go your own way. This simple method allowed the students to rehearse a fundamental principle for a brief communication between two acquaintances, illustrating that a detailed explanation of how we "are" isn't really being sought when someone asks, *How are you?*

The same technique may be used for more comprehensive learning experiences, such as learning what to do, what to buy, and what to wear when you are invited to a Christmas party or wedding. Indeed, most of us learn about it from real-life situations, but such structured learning, especially in times of stress, may be an important step toward rapid acquisition of social skills.

Family Engagement

Sometimes, if the situation allows, it is possible for family members to help one another deal with stress. Family members may work together to provide a less painful process of initial adjustment, especially in cases of refugees or asylum seekers. The main goal of family engagement is to teach social skills and establish the rules that all family members can follow. One family member may have an easier and smoother initial adaptation than the others in the same family. "It was still easier for me to go through stress than for my older family members, brothers and sisters, my parents especially," said an Afghanistan-born young woman. Such people may serve as role models for other members of the family. "We gained a lot from our mother who was an extremely strong person. She was able to be strong in a new environment," an Egypt-born engineer said of his mother. "The problem is that many families are not as lucky as ours." Indeed, sometimes families are preoccupied by their own problems, and they cannot pay attention to coping strategies of their relatives. Family engagement allows families, at least in some cases, to establish understanding and develop mutual concerns among the family members.

Just Ask!

American culture may seem individualistic, but when you need help, you ask for it! As American philosopher William Hocking put it, "We cannot swing on the rope attached only to our own belt." We need something or somebody to hold on to. This may be different from what many people are used to in their homeland, when an old friend will knock at your door because he or she feels that you need aid. Search for help; do not wait too long. You acquire your friends in your home countries naturally through schools you went to and streets you played on. If you have arrived in the United States as an adult, you will have fewer friends initially than you might wish to have. It will seem that adults everywhere have already established their own circle of friends. It can be disappointing to wait in hopes that somebody will befriend you. You may have to make the first move and take this difficult step toward friendship. To paraphrase an old axiom, "If the mountain doesn't go to you, go to the mountain."

One of the authors of this book grew up in a communist country and was persuaded by the media that Americans are greedy and heartless, that they never help their neighbors, and they often abandon their friends when they are helpless. He discovered, however, that this is not true. Without his new friends and their generous help, advice, support, and friendship, his stress could have been more difficult than it was.

Re-Entry Stress

Many students who we interviewed for this book never anticipated that going back home, even for a brief visit, can also cause stressful feelings. **Re-entry stress** is the psychological term for the confusion and frustration that is commonly felt when international students and immigrants return for a visit to their home cultures (Shiraev and Levy 2007).

Similar to accumulated stress, the symptoms of re-entry stress could be either pleasant or disturbing. Surprisingly, people are often less aware of the severity of the emotional stress or surprise because it takes place in a culture that is supposedly familiar. "I anticipated how strange it would be to visit my country after these many years, but I never thought it would be so difficult." This is a common reaction of many who visit their home countries after spending significant time in the United States. Reactions can be emotional, like the one we recorded from a woman born in Burma who returned for a visit after ten years: "The food was different. I had never tasted such awful food in my life. But the worst thing was odors around me." These frustrations are not uncommon. People who have been abroad for a long time often forget how much they have harmonized their lifestyles and attitudes to the norms of the new culture, so going home, even for a visit, means experiencing an acculturation process in reverse. Some develop a sudden distaste for their own countrymen, claiming they either lack a "worldview" or concern themselves too much with trivialities.

Friends and family can also be the root of a great deal of frustration. Returnees often report losing patience with loved ones when they try to talk about their experiences, finding that "no one cares or understands who I am now and what I have learned." People may be surprised to find that their friends are not exactly how they left them. Their former best friends may have found new friends, and what they wear or like in music may be different, which can result in feeling left out. "I was different perhaps because of my music preferences, my interests, the words I used, and definitely my dress code. I was not Bolivian. I was American in their eyes" (K., Bolivia).

The benefit of reverse stress is that it can help individuals who temporarily leave the United States. Upon their return to the U.S., it may become a stimulator toward more rapid acculturation.

Have you experienced this type of reverse stress? If yes, what did you feel? Did your impression of your home country change after you spent some time in the United States?

Think
Critically

Dia (a nickname), 21 years of age, is an Asian-born female and part-time college student. She came to the United States two years ago with her parents. Both her parents are scientists. Dia has a brother who is a 15-year-old high school student. Dia's complaints and concerns are: her English progresses too slowly; she is often frustrated when she does not understand what other people are saying; she has no friends and, therefore, feels extremely lonely; she feels inferior; she believes she does not look like most of the people around her; she even thinks that she looks ugly; she misses her home country, but she does not want to go back; as a source of "escape," she keeps listening to her country's music, reads books in her native language, and watches TV news broadcasts in her native language. Dia wants to adjust, get rid of her anxiety, and overcome her fear of rejection by others, the painful emotions that she hadn't experienced in her home country.

Recommendations for change: Dia needs to recognize that she is experiencing stress. She may be able to improve her situation by deciding to undergo the following changes: First, Dia could reduce her frustration and eliminate her fears by changing her attitudes using social skills training. This technique can rid her of the stimuli that causes her negative tendencies and help her to acquire stimuli that will develop feelings of self-respect and personal satisfaction. Here are some behavioral modification techniques that may be helpful to her.

1. Dia should speak English whenever possible, even at home with her parents and her brother. The more she speaks, the less reluctant to speak she will become.

2. Dia should feel free to ask people to repeat what they say to her. There is nothing embarrassing about asking someone to repeat what was said. There are situations in which U.S.-born-and-raised individuals sometimes do not understand one another.

Question: Continue to compile this list of recommendations for Dia. What could you advise her to do, and how could she achieve these changes?

PART 2

Strategies for Successful Students

The skills that you have acquired to be a successful student in your home country will be helpful as you study in the United States. There will be differences, however—some clear, some not so clear that you will encounter as you learn to navigate through your studies. This section addresses some of the most prominent areas that can help international students adapt to the expectations of most colleges in the United States.

CHAPTER 5

Communicating with Professors

*D*o you remember your favorite teacher, that magnificent person from your high school days? Why did you like him or her? In all probability, you may have enjoyed this person's teaching style. You probably liked the way your favorite teacher spoke, described, and explained the material. And, you probably knew how to talk to him or her, when to ask questions, and how to make certain requests. All in all, you felt happy and comfortable with this teacher. Wouldn't it be wonderful if you could have this teacher in all your classes?

Let us get back to reality. You move, change schools, and change teachers. You must adjust to new people and their styles and methods of teaching, understand their requirements, and learn how to communicate with them. This is true for all college students, but the situation becomes more difficult for those who continue their education in a new country. In the United States, there is a great emphasis on diversity and multiplicity of teaching styles; you have to adjust to professors whose teaching methods, overall attitudes, and ways of communication can be as far apart from one another as the North and South Poles. You cannot expect these professors to change their style or be similar to each other and your expectations. What you must do is adjust to and know how to interact with your college professors. Although much of this knowledge comes with experience, there are basic cultural rules of interaction that every student should know. Some of the rules are cross-cultural. In other words, they may exist in each country in the world, and you will easily find out how similar these rules are. However, there are some practices that are culture-specific and must be learned and understood. This chapter will help you gain knowledge about some of the cultural rules that regulate communications between students and their professors in the United States.

Accept Different Styles and Try to Communicate

Think
Critically

Simone was not very happy with the professor who taught her U.S. History class. She went directly to the history department chair to talk about this course and the professor who was teaching it. When the chairperson asked what the problem was, Simone replied that the professor did not follow the textbook precisely in his lectures. He would ask students to read the text at home; in class, however, he would teach material that was not in the textbook. Meanwhile, the professor also said the exams would cover both the lectures and textbook. Simone was confused. When the chairperson asked Simone if there was anything she wanted to change, she said she wanted the professor to change his teaching style and follow the textbook precisely.

Question: Will Simone succeed in her request? Why or why not?

Many international students are often surprised to learn how different college professors can be in teaching style, grading policies, and general way of thinking. Indeed, all professors are different in terms of how much homework they assign, how much work is required in class, and how well they cooperate with students. A rule established by one professor—like submitting your homework assignments only in double-spaced format—may be not required by another one. There are professors who will require you to do a substantial amount of reading and preparation at home so that you come to class prepared. During lectures, these instructors may occasionally refer to the text but will mostly talk about things that do not appear in it. On the other hand, there are professors who follow the textbook page by page and will not get far from its contents.

You will meet professors who give you the freedom to choose the best strategy for studying for their classes. But you will find professors who will follow a very strict and narrow set of procedures and will demand absolute discipline and organization. Some professors allow their students to improve their grades during the semester. For example, if you take several tests, the lowest score or grade will be eliminated. These professors will offer extra-credit assignments and make-up exams that could boost your grade. Others will not offer any make-up tests or extra-credit work and will never eliminate the lowest test grade. Some professors do not give any credit for attendance, suggesting that being in class is your choice. Others give credit for attendance, which may be critical for your final grade. A lot of this information may appear on the syllabus and/or be discussed the first day of class.

In general, professors follow major guidelines for classroom instruction, however; you should not anticipate that every professor will use the same method of teaching. Therefore, in the case described earlier, Simone cannot anticipate that the department chair would tell the professor how to teach classes and what topics should be included or excluded from lectures. Is there a solution for Simone? Yes, there is. If she prefers to study by the book, she can find another professor who also prefers this type of teaching. These decisions need to be made within the first week or two of classes. As the semester progresses, however, requests for changes most likely will not be allowed.

Talking and Discussing

Think
Critically

Hanna, a student from a Middle Eastern country, has taken three classes with Professor James over a one-year period. When the semester was over, Hanna came to Professor James' office to learn about her grade. "It is interesting," commented the professor. "I now realize that I haven't heard your voice the entire year, not during class discussions, or after class." Hanna smiled in reply: "Yes, I don't talk much."

Question: Do you think that Hanna's quietness was due to her individual style, or is it more likely to be a cultural pattern of behavior typical in many other foreign students?

Some international students remain silent in class and do not participate much in discussions. This can be for number of reasons. Some students believe that their knowledge of the English language is not good enough, and they do not want to embarrass themselves when speaking in front of the class. Others think that they do not know enough about the subject of the lecture. Some say that they do not talk much due to cultural rules of their own country, such as questioning or interrupting a person of higher social rank, which may be considered discourteous.

In the United States, however, talking to your professor and asking questions in class is considered a good sign of your interest in the subject. Your professors are encouraged to communicate with the students, so if you do not want to speak up in class, talk to the professor after class. If you do not feel comfortable talking to the professor alone, another classmate with similar concerns could accompany you. If you have several questions and need detailed comments, ask the professor for a meeting during his or her office hours. It is okay to share your concerns about the class. Any constructive suggestions will not be considered a sign of disrespect for your instructor. Most professors keep a schedule of time open during the week to meet with students; these hours are called "office hours." Most professors list the office hours on the syllabus.

Try to participate in class discussions or ask questions. Such participation will not only improve your communication skills and increase your self-confidence, it will also help professors to explain the topic clearly. Do not be afraid to talk to a professor even if you think that the subject of your conversation might not be important to him or her. Say *hello* to professors when you see them in the library, cafeteria, hallway, or on the street, even though you do not have anything to discuss. Just a smile can make a difference in someone's mood. Remember, your teachers are human beings who have their own concerns, make mistakes, and have good and bad days. They, too, need support, and many of them will appreciate it if you express interest, for example, in their research. It is acceptable to ask questions about where and when they earned their degrees, their current research topics, and the next academic conference they are going to attend. You may also ask your teachers about their family. There is a simple test: If your instructor is willing to talk about his family and children, you can continue the conversation. If he or she does not want to talk about these topics at length, avoid asking further personal questions.

Think
Critically

Can your boss be wrong? This incident took place back in the 1990s. The copilot and engineer of a Korean Air Boeing 747 discovered that something was wrong during the flight: All indicators suggested a problem. However, neither said anything about the problem to the captain, who apparently did not see any danger. Several seconds later, the airplane slammed into the top of a mountain, killing 228 passengers. Investigators established that the crew failed to challenge the captain, showing a traditional respect for authority in command. In other words, they assumed that if the boss did not see the problem, then there was no problem (Phillips 1998). Of course, your classroom is not an airplane, and your professor is not a commander. However, such an attitude may be shared by some students: The professor is always right because he or she is a teacher. What do you think about this attitude? Can you recall situations when your teacher made a mistake? Did you tell anybody about it? Do you remember occasions when you disagreed with your professor? Did you express your disagreement? Please explain.

Bringing Gifts

It is a fine idea to express your appreciation to someone who has spent many hours in the classroom sharing knowledge and skills with you. Are there any customs and rules that regulate the ways you should express your thanks to your teachers? Yes. What are the most and least appropriate ways to convey your gratitude to the professor? If you really enjoyed the semester, you can simply stop by the professor's office and say a few nice words about the course. Some students like to sign a card with a few words of appreciation in it. A postcard with the picture of your hometown or country would be a fine token of respect. Some students bring samples of their ethnic food to share with their teachers. A simple written note, however, will always be an appropriate sign of appreciation.

Never bring expensive gifts. Giving presents is a tradition that exists in every country, but in the United States, people also follow certain rules about giving gifts at work. Such rules of ethical behavior do not encourage American college professors to receive gifts from their students. The professor may feel it is necessary to refuse to accept your gift, and that can be an embarrassing situation for both of you. A student with the best intentions may insist that the gift indicates deep feelings of gratitude to the teacher, which is understandable. However, professional rules of teacher-student communication are different from those that friends establish among themselves. Any gifts offered by a student to the professor ahead of final grades can be considered bribes (exchange for a good grade). Moreover, other students may think of a gift-giver as someone who wants to earn an easy grade with the "purchasing power" of her contributions. Therefore, if the professor refuses to accept a gift, it doesn't mean that he or she is disrespectful of the student. The teacher is simply following professional rules of conduct. What should you do if you really want to express your thankful thoughts to the instructor? Your sincere words will mean more to your professor than any souvenirs.

What is reasonable advice to give Arra regarding that expensive quilt brought from his home country? Do not present it to your professor. Give it to a good friend of yours instead!

To Invite or Not to Invite?

Think Critically

Next week Roberto and Maria, second-year international students and twins, will celebrate their 20th birthday. They have invited several friends to their birthday party, mostly students from the university. Before sending invitations, Roberto and Maria argued about whether or not it would be appropriate to invite their favorite math professor. Roberto pointed out that this professor was always open-minded and friendly with students. However, the semester was far from over. If he were invited, some of the other students might consider this invitation an attempt to get a break on the forthcoming tests.

Question: What should they do: invite or not invite the professor to their celebration?

Most of you want to share your joy with other people you like. In every country, it is natural to invite those people to celebrate good news (and sometimes grieve over bad news) with you. You commonly invite your relatives, friends, and sometimes strangers to share a moment of joy. Would it be a good idea to invite a favorite professor to celebrate with you? The answer is that you can invite anyone you want, but informal contacts between students and professors are not always appropriate. The professor should not show any favoritism to particular students. There are formal and informal rules that American professors must follow in their daily interactions with students, and these rules apply even once you have completed the professor's course.

For example, it would be appropriate to invite your instructor to nearly any organized event on campus. It is always a good idea to send an invitation in advance—at least two or three weeks before the event takes place—so that the invitee is able to include this event in his or her work schedule. Celebrations such as a national holiday, a religious holiday, and an important national date that commemorates your country's history all are appropriate reasons for inviting some of your professors to a meeting or party. A more delicate situation can occur, however, if a celebration is held in your dormitory, apartment, house, picnic area, restaurant, or any other place off-campus. Professors, of course, make a final determination about what is proper and what is not, and will make a final decision about whether to attend a celebration.

Of course, certain private events will take place without the presence of faculty members. Among them are your birthday or the birthday of your boyfriend, girlfriend, husband, or wife; arrivals or departures of your relatives (even though they might insist on meeting with your professors); and any regular parties that you organize. On the other hand, it is always a fine idea to invite faculty members to attend a sports event. Some professors never miss the opportunity to play basketball, soccer, or football with their students. Do not forget about chess or other board games.

As to Roberto and Maria's dilemma, good advice will be to let their professor know that they are going to celebrate their 20th birthday. Rather than request your professor's presence at the party, however, invite your friends instead.

To Contact or Not to Contact?

Think
Critically

Shandra is happy, outgoing, and optimistic. She enjoys her study in America, has many wonderful friends, and is always ready to help when somebody needs her assistance or just a few kind words. She likes to share good news with friends and usually spends at least one hour a day sending and receiving email. She has several mailing lists. One contains the names of her parents and other family members in Brazil. Another list contains names of her friends, former classmates in several countries around the world. Her third mailing list contains names of her friends and acquaintances from school. Shandra loves to send copies of messages to everyone on her mailing lists with recent updates, jokes, interesting pieces of information, discussion topics, and some news that she thinks are related to business administration, her major and future specialty. Recently she added to this list several names of her favorite professors that she thinks would enjoy reading her messages.

Question: Was it a good idea to add the names of her professors to one of her mailing lists?

Although the telephone today remains a very important source of communication, most American professors use email to exchange information and news. Only a few years ago this form of communication was considered entertaining and amusing. But that has changed. Today it is becoming increasingly difficult to use email because there are too many messages being received and not enough time to go through all of them! On an average day, a college professor receives from 20 to 30 electronic messages from colleagues and school administrators. Moreover, if a professor teaches three classes with 30 students in each of them, his or her potential for messages can be in the hundreds every day. How can you be "email effective"? In other words, how can you get the most from your electronic communication with professors? There are several tips that can make your interpersonal communications more efficient.

If you have questions for your professor about the course you are currently taking, make sure that these questions are not already answered in the syllabus or other course documents. If you have a question about a recent lecture, be sure that the question is short so that the answer, too, can be brief. Unless your professor has agreed to discuss some topics with you at a great length, please respect his or her time: sometimes it is easier and takes less time to ask a question and receive an answer in person. To simplify the professor's work, always design your message so that the professor can easily recognize who the sender is.

There is a common communication error that many students commit:

> "Professor, this is J., we spoke today; I'm taking your class. Will you be so kind and tell me my grade for the last test?"

Even though the professor recognizes your face, it is quite likely that he or she may not remember what class you are taking, especially if he or she teaches two or three sections of the same course. Therefore, at the beginning of the message, put your name and the course you are taking, including the course section and the time the class meets. Be clear in the subject line of the email; make sure it communicates what you want or need. A blank subject line will not attract the professor's attention. Try to ask questions about your grade when the professor has an easy access to the grade book or the computer file. Sometimes this can be done more efficiently in person after class or during office hours.

Every professor will probably explain what kind of electronic communication he expects to establish with the students during the semester. Some professors allow students to request their grades via email. On the contrary, some may ask you to do it in person during office hours. Some professors will not mind sending you copies of class assignments and other handouts distributed in class. Others will not do that under any circumstances. In any case, if you have doubts about the professor's communication style, ask this question after class or send a message. Your professor will appreciate such a request.

Try to understand that in the vast majority of situations, your electronic communication with professors should be formal. It is different from your electronic interaction with friends to whom you can send messages spontaneously as soon as you have an idea. Do not send your professor jokes, funny stories, and other interesting—from your viewpoint—items that are flying in cyberspace. If you think that you have found an extremely interesting piece of information, save it on your computer, and then tell your professor about it. If he or she is interested, then send it. If you need your professor's suggestions or other help, it is always better to make an appointment rather than send an email. During the appointment, the professor can spend more time and can offer you more options than he or she can do via email.

We would advise Shandra not to include her professors' names in her mailing lists. If she really wanted to do this, she should ask their permission first. It is important to respect other people's privacy.

✎ For Class Discussion

Consider this message left on a professor's answering machine:

> "Hello, professor, this is Ahmad calling; could you tell me what the status of my request is? We spoke yesterday and you asked me to call today."

Can you find several mistakes that Ahmad made in his assertion? First, he did not mention his last name. Second, Ahmad failed to remind the professor of the nature of the request. The professor may not remember his conversation with Ahmad. It is helpful to remind the person of the topic of your previous conversation and the nature of your request. Professors have more than a hundred students in any one semester. Imagine, for example, that you are going to pick up your friend at the airport tomorrow and will have to miss a test. You talked to your professor in advance, and she asked that you call her today to clarify what you are supposed to do about the missed exam. Compose an "ideal" telephone message you would leave on the professor's answering machine.

Rules of Address

Think
Critically

The door to my office was open, but the student knocked anyway. "May I come in?" he asked cautiously.

"Yes," I replied, "Come in. Sit down, please. How can help you?"

The student entered my small office, smiled, and said quietly: "Dr. Eric, I have a question for you."

The question was simple, and I quickly gave the answer. What was interesting about the situation was the way the student addressed me. He called me "Dr. Eric." That's a form of address I haven't heard very often. Maybe my last name is too difficult to pronounce correctly? Or maybe it is not difficult to articulate but difficult to remember? Or, is this a new, popular style of address?

Question: Is it appropriate to address your professor by his or her first name?

Some students are uncertain about how to address their professors. Should I use their first name, or last name, or both? How do I use academic and professional titles when addressing other people? In addition, for some students it may become tough to pronounce some professors' last names. If a name is difficult to pronounce, the situation creates additional difficulties: fear of embarrassment, fear of rejection, and worry about possible criticism.

Not many professors in the United States who teach undergraduate students prefer to be called by their first names. Under most circumstances, it is preferable to use your teacher's last name, regardless of how difficult it may be to pronounce. If your professor is a man, you can call him Mr. Browning or Mr. Wong. If your professor is a woman you should call her Ms. Smithers or Ms. Nicholson. For example, you can freely call your instructor *professor* and include the last name, for example, Professor Gonzales. If the instructor has a doctorate degree, it is common to call him or her *doctor,* again including the last name: Doctor Barnard or Doctor Bean.

Many students—especially from Arabic and Latin American countries—use the instructor's title and first name. For example, they would say *Dr. John* or *Professor Susan.* This is not a common form of address in direct communications in the United States, although most professors will likely accept it.

When you start a conversation or want to get your instructor's attention, bear in mind that you are not talking to a stranger. Introductory words such as *hey* or *wait a minute* are not the best starters for your conversation with any professor. It is always a sign of respect to use your professor's title and name when addressing him or her. For example, you can say, *Excuse me, Professor Smith* or *I have a question, Doctor Deregowski.*

Pay attention to how your teacher's name is spelled. Most professors will not pay special attention to whether or not you correctly spell their names; however, some instructors are very sensitive to how their names appear on paper or in an electronic message. So double-check the spelling of your instructor's name on your assignments or written messages.

When you call your professor on the phone, always say your name and class you are taking (do the same in your email messages). Remind the person you are calling of the nature of your question or request.

Personal Problems: To Share or Not to Share?

Think Critically

When Tina appeared in the professor's office she was visibly upset. Moreover, when Tina began to talk, her voice was breaking and she was about to cry. "Professor," she said, "I need your help and advice. My parents want me to go back to my home country because they think that my education is not going well here. I am not getting good grades, and this is the only thing they care about. They do not care about how I would feel if I leave this place. I made so many great friends here. I know that I can improve the grades very soon; but it takes time, and my parents do not want to wait. Please tell me what to do: oppose my parents and stay here or go back to my home country? Please let me know. I really like your lectures."

Question: Is Tina making a wise decision by talking to her professor about a private issue? Does a college professor have an obligation to help students who experience personal problems?

When there is a tough decision to make, many people usually seek help and advice from their relatives and close friends. However, when you live away from home, you may not have many people who you can talk to and share your concerns or pain or to whom you can simply complain about something you dislike. Generally speaking, if a problem occurs, try to talk to the person who you think is able to solve this problem. For example, if you think that your math professor did not grade your exam justly, the first step is to speak to the professor in person and ask him or her to explain how your test was graded. After such a conversation, in most cases, the problem is solved: The professor may find an error in grading or explain to you why you received this particular score. If you are still not satisfied with the way your problem is being solved or the way your request is handled, you can speak to one of the college's administrators. Almost every employee on campus, including faculty members, has a supervisor who is supposed to help you solve the problem, if it persists.

Almost every professor will be willing to listen to you carefully and offer practical help or advice. The main focus of your dialogue with the professor should center on the course you are taking, your academic program, and how these fit with your career or future plans. You have to differentiate, however, between two types of problems that you may encounter, each requiring a different approach. First, there are formal or organizational problems that have to do with the college or some aspect of its operation. For example, issues related to your visa status or your financial situation should not be discussed with your professor. These should be only discussed with your ISA. Always go to your ISA first with any concern about anything related to college. The ISA will refer you to others if he or she cannot help.

Second, there are personal problems that are mostly concerned with your interpersonal relationships with the people in your life. Refer now to the box, read the scenarios, and decide which are "official" and which are "personal."

✎ A Class Assignment

Indicate which of the problems below are official (O) and should be addressed through official channels at your college and which are personal (P). Discuss your answers in class.

1. You have broken up with your friend and ask your professor's advice on whether to see this person again.

2. You got a parking ticket and you do not want to pay it because you think that campus police gave you the ticket by mistake. You ask your professor to intervene and help you resolve the situation.

3. Your parents told you to select computer science as your major. However, you want to choose biology. You ask your professor what major you should declare.

4. You have a problem with a student who verbally assaulted you not long ago and threatened to create more problems for you in the future. You ask your professor's advice.

5. You have a problem with your roommate. She is messy, noisy, and always talks to you when you are working on homework assignments. You ask your professor to have a word with your roommate.

6. The library wants you to pay a fine for returning a book past its due date. You ask your professor to solve the situation.

Did you determine that the Situations 1, 3, and 5 are personal problems? You can talk about them to your professor but you should not expect that he or she will give you a suggestion about what to do. He or she is not in a position to give you advice. Do not expect that your professor will say a lot to a question related to your relationship with your parents, siblings, or friends. The student counseling center is the best place to seek help related to your personal problems. Situations 2, 4, and 6 require some formal action to resolve them. Your instructor can tell you what official channels you should use and can help you to find the right office.

What kind of personal information can you disclose to your college professor, and should you expect help in these situations? Professors are not permitted to share with anyone else the private information you disclose to them. Understand, however, that professors are not marriage counselors or psychotherapists (although some of them may hold these titles). The most a professor can do is to listen to you and give a general opinion. Of course, professors will be happy to give you a specific suggestion if your request is a course-related one. Ask them what book to buy or what article to look for, and they will be happy to elaborate on that subject.

Most schools have counseling centers your professor may refer you to that address problems that are out of his or her area of expertise. If you begin to have personal issues and need to talk to someone, begin with a counselor. Also, you may want to speak with your International Student Advisor first for a reference.

Negotiating Your Grade

Think Critically

Palar was disappointed with the grade he received for the sociology class. At the beginning of the semester he anticipated receiving an A. When the grades were posted, he found that he was given a C. Palar decided to talk to the professor. The reason? He didn't like the grade. He knew that during the semester he was not getting good test scores in this class. He also remembered he missed several classes that could also have lowered his grade. Nevertheless, Palar was very optimistic about having a conversation with the professor. He knew that he could do much better in this class. He also knew he was a great negotiator. In his home country, his teachers told him many times that he could become a fine businessman because he knew how to bargain. In his brief career, he had learned to negotiate almost anything, anywhere—at a farm market, car dealership, travel agency, and many other places. Palar thought that if he asked the professor to change the grade from a C to an A, after some negotiation, the professor would give him a B.

Question: Is it a good idea to discuss your grade with a professor, or is it absolutely inappropriate?

Some people mistakenly presume that college education is a kind of business and professors are entrepreneurs who "take" money from students and "give" an education and grades in exchange. Some believe that for the money students give for their education they are entitled to negotiate the outcome, or grades. It is not that Palar cannot ask his professor why the grade was a *C*. He can. Most professors keep students informed about their grade status throughout the semester. In this case, Palar knew that his class performance was far from satisfactory. However, he believed, that like everything else in life, his grade could be negotiated. Through the use of his communication skills and a great deal of aggressiveness, he anticipated that he could persuade the professor to change the grade.

Palar has made a mistake to assume that college grades can be negotiated between students and professors. The rules are fair and square: Grades are not supposed to be negotiated. Professors give grades according to their grading system, not according to their feelings or what some students tell them they want to get. If a student believes that there is a computation error in a professor's calculations, he or she should mention it and ask the teacher to set aside a few minutes and recalculate the grade. For this purpose, keep copies of your graded tests and homework assignments. There cannot be any other reasons, however, for you to ask your professor to change the grade.

The end of the term is not the time to ask for help. As soon as you find yourself falling behind, you should seek help immediately. Contact your ISA, and work on a plan to help you catch up. Your ISA will be able to identify support options like tutoring or lab help, and they can consider other options with you like withdrawing and completing the semester on a reduced course load. Do not make these choices on your own! Dropping below a full-time load can have serious implications for your visa status. Your ISA must be involved for any course load reduction.

Think
Critically

Here are reasons that some students give for trying to negotiate their grades with the professor. Take a look at the explanations and see why these reasons cannot be accepted as legitimate requests for a grade change.

Professor, I attended all your lectures, submitted all the required assignments, and took all the tests. However, my grade is not an A. I think I deserve a better grade.

Why the grade will not be changed: Even though one takes all the tests and fulfills all the requirements for the course, the final grade is based on the quality of the submitted assignments and tests, not on one's positive attitude and good intentions. There are plenty of sports teams, as an example, that play all the games but still may finish last in the season.

Professor, I never get grades lower than A (or B). Therefore, I should receive an A (B) in your class too.

Why the grade will not be changed: Your past performance is not necessarily an indicator of what grade you will achieve in your next class.

Professor, this semester was very difficult for me. I was taking five classes. I did not have much time to prepare for the tests in your class. However, I enjoyed your teaching method, and I think I really improved my skills and acquired new knowledge. I think I can improve my grade if you give me an extra week.

Why the grade will not be changed: Every student has a choice before the semester begins to take more or fewer classes. You are responsible for the additional pressure you place on yourself by taking more classes than you can handle. In addition, by requesting an extra week, the student is asking for a break that the other students will not have.

Professor, without a good grade in your class I will not be able to apply for a graduate school (transfer to another school; apply for financial aid; etc.). Please understand my situation and change my grade.

Why the grade will not be changed: Colleges and universities are not designed to give away grades because someone wants to go to a different school or pursue a particular career. If one's grades are lower than expected, the student can always retake some of the classes to improve the grades.

Think Critically

Robert was very interested in the history of the American Revolution. He came to his professor and said he would like to learn more about this period in history. He also said that he might think about majoring in history. The professor said he would be very happy to chat with Robert tomorrow afternoon during lunch. The professor made an appointment to meet with Robert in the cafeteria at 12:40 PM the next day. Robert agreed to be there. Robert could not have anticipated how busy he would be the next morning. When he ran to meet his professor, he realized he was late. He was thinking: "If I'm late 10 or 20 minutes, that will be okay. The teacher is a junior professor, and it is no problem to be late for a meeting with him. One has some time flexibility with the middle-aged professors, but one has to be very careful and try not to be late for meetings with senior professors."

Question: What was correct and incorrect in Robert's thinking?

Keeping Appointments

The word a*ppointment* is a very popular word in America. Listen to what other people say, and you will hear this word mentioned often in their conversations. From the beginning of their lives, people in the United States are taught to schedule appointments. If you want to meet someone and discuss business or business-related problems, you typically have to agree on both the place and the time of such a meeting (see Chapter 4, page 54, on acculturated stress). Some professors do not have to schedule appointments with their students because they can receive students during office hours. If you need to see your professor outside of scheduled office hours, an appointment is a better option than just trying to drop in. An email request for an appointment is a good option.

Professors do more than teach classes. Their day is filled with various activities, from preparing and reading new literature related to their classes, to grading papers and exams and reviewing lecture notes. Most professors have scholarly research to do as well. Some do their research in their offices; some of them spend a substantial amount of time in the library; some of them have to go off-campus. Professors also attend meetings, meet with other professors and school officials, write reports, and help graduate students and guests scholars. Therefore, it is highly unlikely that your professor will be able to talk to you outside of class whenever you show up at his or her office; you should make an appointment.

The most convenient time for you to talk to the professor might be before or after class. These times are most likely not good times for your professor, however, unless he or she has scheduled office hours at that time period. It is easy to understand why. Right before class, the instructors would like to think about the lecture, read over any new information, and make copies and prepare handouts and other class materials. In addition, the professor may have plans after class, so there is not much time to answer your questions. To avoid confusion or disappointment, always ask the professor if he or she has some time available to answer your questions. Do not keep your professor long after class, unless he or she has said it is all right. Your teacher may have another class or an important appointment in several minutes.

Robert's "theory" about how late he could be for the appointment being dependent on the professor's status disregards simple rules of courtesy. Regardless of your professor's age and rank, if you show up just one minute past the appointment time, you are late.

Even though cultural differences in time perception exist, we might begin to consider that many contemporary technological developments, including the expansion of television and the Internet, as well as the increasing complexity of modern life, might make cultural differences in how people perceive time less significant than they have been in the past. "Real time" communication and the global economy have brought cultures much closer together. This may or may not be true. Do you think that in the contemporary world people treat their time more or less in the same way? Do you think that instead of emphasizing cultural differences, we can see that there are different individual characters in every culture: There are people who are precise and disciplined, and there are those who are always late?

Asking for a Letter of Support (Recommendation)

Think
Critically

After finishing her two-year education at local college, Laura decided to transfer to a small private university. Before starting the transfer, she needed to collect a recommendation letter from one of her former professors. Laura decided to ask Professor Brown to write the letter because she did well in this professor's class. She checked Professor Brown's schedule and waited to talk to her near the classroom following an evening class she was teaching. After all the students were gone, she approached the professor with a smile, and said: "Professor Brown, do you remember me? Thank you, I have a favor to ask. I need a letter of recommendation from you. Can you give it to me on Monday? I know today is Friday; I hope it is enough time for you to write this letter. Thank you again."

Question: What mistakes did Laura make in her request for a letter of support from Professor Brown?

When you plan to transfer to another college or want to apply for a graduate school or job, you will have to obtain and submit letters of recommendation, often called letters of support. These letters need to be written by professors or people who can verify your academic abilities; friends cannot write these letters. Many students believe that to obtain such a letter, they must simply go to somebody they know and ask for the recommendation. However, once someone agrees to give you the letter, you should take some extra steps and help your professor to prepare a good document for you. First, prepare a brief memo to your professor that contains your name, your major, the class or classes you are taking or have already taken with this professor, your major accomplishments (awards or other academic achievements), and your professional experience, if any. The application process may include specific guidelines for the letter, which you should pass on to the letter writer. Do not forget to list any internships and other forms of activities. Inform the professor about where the letter is being submitted. Do not come to the professor with a request on the same day that you need the letter. Give your professor at least several days, and preferably a week, to prepare the letter for you. You can help your professor by reminding him or her who you are, what you have accomplished, and what purpose the letter will serve. You should not be shy about asking for a letter of recommendation from your professor or anyone else at the college who can write about your strengths and attributes. If you were involved in activities outside of your classes, the coordinators or advisors of those activities would be good sources. Don't forget about your ISA; your ISA is often the best person to summarize your accomplishments.

Recording Your Accomplishments

Think Critically

Eva was approached by a school official who said that there was a job available for her next semester. It was a desirable and long-anticipated job for Eva because she would be able to work on campus and she could adjust her work hours to her class schedule. Eva was asked to prepare a resume that included all of her accomplishments and to bring it in the next day. Eva went home and opened a new file on her computer. She began to realize how difficult it was to write about herself. Accomplishments? Achievements? There were so many interesting events in her life, but she seemed to have a hard time putting everything together.

Question: When should you start working on a resume?

If you plan to continue your education or to work in the United States, you will need to have a resume or one- to two-page autobiography. Many students pay little or no attention to their resume until they have to submit one. Certain rules apply when putting together a resume. Formal rules for resumes can be found in books or on the Internet. Since a good resume takes more than a few minutes to prepare, begin the process as soon as your first day in college. Record in a notebook things that you do as a student: Write information about awards you receive, concerts and sports tournaments you organize, student conferences you participated in, membership in student groups on campus, volunteer activities, tutoring of other students, internships, and articles written. To be more competitive than other students, include specific results and accomplishments, not just the meetings you attend or groups in which you were just a formal member.

Details, Details, Details

Throughout this textbook, we strongly suggest that every student who goes through an adjustment period should look around and see what other people are doing. We often learn by imitation. Sometimes these lessons are helpful. Learning from others can be quick, useful, and profitable. Sometimes, however, we observe examples of what we should not do, and sometimes these are more valuable. Most students around you are mature, polite, considerate, and helpful, but some student behavior should not be imitated. Some practical suggestions about what is considered to be appropriate behavior that will help you to be effective in your interaction with faculty members follows.

✓ Never talk loudly with your friends in class during lecture. Exercise your freedom of expression when the professor asks you to express your opinion. Even though you think that you are not talking aloud, the professor can hear your conversation, which may disturb the lecture. Moreover, students who are sitting near you may also be disturbed by your chatting. Remember, the classroom is for learning and not for exchanging comments about yesterday's game or your new friends.

✓ Everybody is very busy. We know that we are not supposed to be late for class. If you are late, try not to be disruptive. As you enter the classroom, do not walk slowly in front of the professor and the entire class. Try to avoid attention and find a seat in the back or a corner.

✓ Never start your conversation with the professor by saying, *Hey, how did you like my last paper?* or *What can you say about how I did on my exam?* Although most professors have good memories, they may not remember what you wrote in the last paper or what grade you got on the last test. For such questions, see the instructor in his or her office where he or she can easily check the record.

✓ If you make an important request to a professor, make it in writing—for example, if you need a letter of recommendation, want your professor to give you an extra-credit assignment, or want to invite him or her to attend a celebration. Remember that a brief email in many situations is better than a long conversation.

✓ Try not to speak loudly with your friends in your native language in the presence of the professor with whom you are speaking. There is nothing wrong with speaking one's language. When several people are involved in a conversation, everyone is entitled to understand what the participants are saying. Speaking a language your teacher does not understand may be interpreted as disrespect.

✓ Many students grab something to eat before going to class. If your food contains fresh onion or garlic, consider eating it after you return home from school. Garlic and onion smell can be offensive and may distract the people to whom you are talking, including your professor. Professors may not mention your garlic or onion breath; however, they will run away from you.

 ## A Homework Assignment

When we interact with other people, we pay attention to how they use their bodies, hands, and faces to convey their thoughts and emotions. The speaker's body language helps us understand a person better. Whether you were born in Mexico, India, Vietnam, or Indonesia, you understand similar signs of body language across cultures (Shiraev and Levy 2007). One quick smile and you understand that the professor is joking. A smirk may indicate that she is being sarcastic. By shrugging shoulders, a person shows that he does not know something.

There are differences, however, in how we use body language, and interpretations differ across cultures. One example is how we position our bodies when we speak to another person. Touching is more common in the cultures around the Mediterranean Sea and in some Slavic nations than it is in the United States. Latinos may interact using smaller physical distances compared to people from Japan, East Asia, Western Europe, and the United States, who enjoy up to three feet of personal space.

Assignment: Observe your professors' movements, facial expressions, and entire body language. See how they shift their eyes, where they point their finger, how often and how high they wave their arms, when they scratch their head, and so forth. Try to find similarities between how these people and people in your home country express themselves. Discuss your findings in class.

CHAPTER 6

Tips for Writing in College

America is a culture of written communications. Invitations, memos, announcements, and reminders are typed and placed daily into people's mailboxes or attached to bulletin boards. Americans are well connected to the Internet, and email is part of most people's daily lives. People write to each other on Internet chat rooms, blogs, and they visit each other on myspace®. Written tests and written assignments are the core of college evaluation systems. Oral exams, often practiced in other countries, are administered in only a few schools in the United States. As a result, your success in college will be measured, in part, by how well you write since much of the work done to complete all classes will be written. This chapter explains how to prepare for written assignments and research papers. Some important tips of successful paper writing will be discussed and several principles of analytical thinking—a key tool to effective discovery, examination, and interpretation of facts—will be introduced.

Written assignments are one of the most challenging activities in college. Do not get the impression that people who attended American elementary, middle, and high schools and who have spoken English since birth have a tremendous advantage over you. Writing, even for native speakers of English, is a difficult skill that one can work a lifetime to master. It may be that it is sometimes easier for native English speakers to understand professors, take notes, and quickly grasp what is required in written assignments. It may also appear that it is easier for them to put their thoughts into writing. But do not be discouraged. You have both the skills and opportunities to write well and be competitive. If you accept the following suggestions and work on your writing skills every day, you will definitely become a better student!

The Research Paper: Preparation Strategies

When you write poetry, you use a free flow of associations to link the images in a pleasing way. In verse, you convey your feelings and appeal to the feelings and imagination of the reader. Research papers written for history, sociology, psychology, political science, and many other subjects are quite different. Professors normally provide you with some instructions and guidelines on what is expected in their writing assignments. Every professor may have a unique set of expectations, requirements, and recommendations for student papers. However, there are certain principles of paper-writing that most American professors expect every student to follow. Thus, for most assignments, you will be asked to work independently and express your independent judgment based on empirical materials available to you, including confirmed facts, statistical information, expert judgment, opinion polls, and other data. It is also commonly anticipated that your research paper will be a rational and critical evaluation of the suggested topic. It is expected that you cite references, that is, name the source of your facts. If you do not give credit to the people whose work you are citing, it is considered plagiarism. Most colleges and universities have harsh penalties for this kind of cheating. We will discuss this issue later.

Typically, a paper will require you to do one or more of the following.

Fact-Finding

You must search for, locate, and demonstrate an understanding of the facts or data requested in the assignment. Your job is to confirm a theory or an existing tendency. You do not have to argue about the suggested topic; your job is to demonstrate, prove, or disprove something.

> ## ☆ A Useful Tip
>
> Before starting your work on the research paper, ask yourself, "Do I understand the assignment? What is the purpose of the writing? What am I trying to accomplish here? Do I know where to find facts and ideas for the paper? How much time do I want to spend on the paper, and how much time do I have?" Asking these questions should help you to choose the most appropriate and relevant strategy. Many schools have tutoring or writing centers to help you with your papers. Use these services! Also, make sure that you take the required English and math courses early in your program. These courses will help you perform better in the rest of your classes.

Examples:

(1) Find some facts about the divorce rates in the United States.

(2) Who were the most active voters in the United States in the 2000 and 2004 elections: men or women?

Decision-Making

For some assignments, two or more options are proposed, and you have to choose and defend one of the proposed alternatives.

Examples:

(1) Do you think that it is a government's responsibility to provide health insurance to all citizens, or is it each individual's responsibility?

(2) What is more important for an immigrant: (a) to integrate into American culture, (b) to preserve his or her cultural identity, or (c) both?

Problem-Solving

These assignments require you to find your own answer to the question or problem introduced in the assignment. Unlike in decision making, you have to come up with your own theory, explanation, or idea. Therefore, you must support your answer with arguments. You can use at least two strategies. First is the **inductive** method, where you collect information and then offer your explanation. The **deductive** method requires you first to have an answer, a hypothesis; then you collect information in order to confirm that your answer is correct.

Examples:

(1) Why are the crime rates higher in big cities than in small towns?

(2) Choose a theory that, in your opinion, gives the most reasonable explanation of prejudice.

Written Assignments: Basic Elements

Typically, unless the professor requires something else, your paper may contain several common elements. First, you have to write an introduction in which you briefly describe the goal of your paper: a theory you defend, evidence you find, or opinion that you want to express. It is fine to use a quote, proverb, or saying that reflects and conveys your main idea or point. Next, you describe the method of your investigation (book review, newspaper review, Internet search, interviews you conducted yourself, and so on). Do not forget to identify and describe the sample: how many books or articles you reviewed, people you interviewed, websites you searched through, or television shows you watched. Then present your arguments in several paragraphs. Each paragraph should represent a particular idea, explanation of the idea, or description of somebody or something. Usually, the first sentence in the paragraph represents the main idea. The remainder of the paragraph expands on the idea. An example is:

> **Researchers have identified considerable evidence that environment is related to the health status of individuals.** There are large national differences in life expectancy, but, in general, socioeconomic conditions and life expectancy are positively correlated. For instance, African Americans are three times as likely as Caucasians to be poor, and their life expectancy is six years short of the Caucasians' life expectancy according to the U.S. National Center for Health Statistics (Shiraev and Sobel 2006). Illness and poverty are linked across countries. For example, although the overall AIDS-related death rate has declined, the death rate for women continues to rise, particularly among those who are more likely to be poor compared to other groups. (U.S. Department of Health and Human Services 2007.)

Finally, sum up your thoughts in a conclusion. State whether the goal described in the introduction was achieved. Sometimes it is a good idea to include your comments about how difficult or easy it was to work on the assignment, what new things you learned, and some new ideas you have about future research. In your conclusion, if it is appropriate, suggest where and how your data should be or could be used.

How and Where to Find Facts and Data

Your work on the paper should begin with the research for available and credible literature and other sources of information. The more credible the sources supporting your work, the stronger your argument and paper.

- ✓ Search for books and journals. Besides the library at your college or university, you can visit any public library in your area, including county libraries. Most library services are free except photocopying. Although some journals can be found online, you will need to cite some books, and many of these can only be found in a library.
- ✓ Search for newspaper articles. Most newspapers have easily accessible websites where the most current reports are published. In

addition, many libraries have software provided by major regional or national newspapers with articles published since the early 1990s.

✓ Search for databases on the Internet. There are plenty of publicly available databases on the Internet. Your school may also have specialized databases accessible only through the school network. Consult with your library for instructions.

✓ Television is usually not a prime source of research information; however, some fact-finding can be done there. Major networks and local stations (see Chapter 10 on the Media) have websites and usually publish transcripts of the most recent programming.

✓ Avoid citing from websites like Wikipedia or other non-credible sites.

Interactive Reading

Reading the materials you have collected for the paper is an interactive process. You might find some ideas that are useful and others not quite so. You might misunderstand one theory and be inspired by another; you can agree or disagree with your findings. You can easily help yourself to remember any associations, ideas, and sometimes emotions that you experienced when you were reading the materials by preparing a set of symbols (see below). The easiest symbols are the exclamation mark (!) and the question mark (?) next to material you are reading. The "!" almost always indicates that the sentence before it stands for something important, interesting, or meaningful. It identifies something you shouldn't miss when you start writing your paper. The "?" could indicate your misunderstanding of a concept. If you put it in front of a sentence, you could easily recognize that you should get additional information about this sentence. Many students might use only these two symbols. However, there could be other interactive marks. You can write these symbols on the draft, printed copies of the materials you are working with, or in your notes. Please: **Never write in library books or journals.**

Possible Symbols

!   This is a very important definition (description, theory, story, etc.).

?   I don't understand this. It needs further clarification.

Y   Yes, I agree with the author; I have the same thoughts!

N   No, I disagree with the author; I do not think he or she is right.

Q   Question. I will have to ask my professor about this. Is it true?

M   More information is needed. I would like to learn more about this topic or case.

Example:

Left Margin   **Text (or your notes)**

Q	<u>Some . . . psychologists</u> studied the influence of birth order on the individual's behavior. The first child is almost always forced into second place by
?	the birth of a little brother or sister. This might develop a sense of <u>inferiority</u> and protest against both the parents and the new sibling. Alfred Adler wrote that the first-born child finds himself deprived of the privileged position in
?	the family after the birth of the sibling. The first-born becomes <u>resentful</u> and insecure. He may develop a distrust of people and will try to secure his future against other sudden events in the future. The child becomes cau-
YM	tious and even <u>conservative</u> in his approach to life.

The symbols on the left margin indicate the following:

Q stands for a question you will ask about the names of psychologists who studied birth order and its influence on behavior; it might also mean that you didn't recognize the names in the text and need more information.

? The two question marks indicate that there are two words (*inferiority* and *resentful*) you are not familiar with: you can guess their meanings but need exact translations. You will find them in a dictionary.

YM indicates that you agree with this statement (Yes, it is true, I am more conservative and cautious than my younger brothers) and would like to learn more about the subject.

How to Improve Understanding of the Written Material

In some classes professors will ask you to read a minimum of 100 pages a week. In other classes, your reading assignments will be even more difficult and time-consuming. Working on a typical assignment, you may be required to go through dozens of websites and read more than several long articles. Reading comprehension is crucial to your success in college. There are several things you can do to improve your reading.

When you read a report from a newspaper and want to include some ideas from the report in your paper, it is important that you write down the most essential points of the article. This is done so that you can access the information more efficiently when the time comes to use it in your paper. To do this successfully, you have to learn how to generalize and categorize the information you are reading.

To convert a long paragraph into a shorter transcript, you have to recognize the most important points and the main ideas of the paragraph. Try to consolidate ideas: compress three, four, or five sentences into one.

Example of a thought compression:

Text says:

Every person has his or her own theory according to which there is a balance between what one does and what one gets for it. We get angry when the balance is challenged by someone's actions. You get angry when you feel that you are entitled to get a promotion, but, instead, someone else gets promoted. You feel angry when the governor promised to lower your taxes but ignores his promise four years later. Or, you get angry when you are waiting in a long line to buy a ticket and somebody sneaks into the line right in front of you.

This is what appears in your notes:

We are angry when we feel entitled to something but do not obtain it: For instance, one sneaks into the line in front of you.

Like many of our other skills, thought compression can be learned, practiced, and significantly improved. If you want to succeed at thought compression, you have to practice this skill continuously regardless of how well you speak English.

✎ Class Exercises

Convert each of the following paragraphs about prejudice into one sentence. Write the summary sentence after the paragraph. Hint: Identify the main point or major idea of each paragraph.

1. Specialists argue about whether or not it is possible to overcome prejudice, whether or not it has always existed, and if it will continue to exist in human beings. Social scientists are divided on the issue: Some remain optimistic, while others take a pessimistic view on prejudice and its origins. Let us briefly examine their arguments, both in defense and against prejudice.

2. Pessimists argue that prejudice is a logical generalization based on facts and individual experiences. Well-educated and uneducated people have the potential to be prejudiced. Prejudice is a form of self-defense; if you get rid of it, you disarm yourself. That there could be social equity is a sweet myth that is nice to place in political fairy tales. If social conditions outline the way you think, you will always be disappointed because somebody will always have more than you do, and there will always be somebody who will try to get something from you. You will always protect what you have and blame those who frighten you.

3. The other group of pessimists suggests that prejudice is indeed an irrational fear. It is built into our psyche from the beginning of our lives. Aggression, violence, destruction, and humiliation have their deep roots in our unconscious mind. We can change the direction of aggression but not aggression itself. Our thinking is schematic; therefore, we will always perceive this world as a continuous existence and struggle between opposites. Like day and night, hot and cold, men and women, good and evil, rich and poor—we will always think of the world in these categories.

4. Optimists challenge pessimists by saying that prejudice is an irrational attitude based on ignorance and fear. When you open your mind, read, watch, listen, learn, educate yourself, and get rid of your irrational fears, you will reduce your prejudice. Cross-cultural interaction makes people less prejudiced. Interpersonal contacts, joint projects, international exchanges, and continuous communications all bring people closer to each other, make people friendlier to each other. Situations that are especially helpful are those in which people of different cultural backgrounds try to overcome obstacles together.

5. The optimists also say that social conditions direct your way of thinking. Whenever people become really equal, whenever they stop the discrimination of one group against another, the justification of prejudice will inevitably disappear. People compete for resources. If there is nothing to compete for, if nobody is left behind, then this will be the end of prejudice.

A Homework Assignment

Select a front-page article from a local newspaper. Read the article and, using three to four short sentences, write the article's content. Refer to the article, and find out if you missed any important ideas or whether you interpreted them correctly. Try this activity with a friend and compare notes.

You can choose a more difficult assignment if you have a VCR, TEVO, or DVR. Find a network that broadcasts the news. Record the news. At the same time, take notes and follow the fast-speaking news anchors. (You may skip the commercials.) After ten minutes, stop recording and taking notes. Rewind the tape or DVD, and compare the recorded news with your transcript. Note any important elements you missed. Analyze what was the most difficult for you to do. If you work on this assignment with a friend, compare your notes.

Spell or Misspell?

When you write, do you always have to spell correctly, or can you take an easier approach and check the spelling later when you have the time? Some people prefer to write everything correctly from the start. This accuracy helps them to be organized and precise. Other people feel better when they do not pay attention to the spelling because they want to be focused on what they write and do not want to forget their thoughts. They prefer to check the spelling later. Of course, you must check spelling before you submit your paper to your professor—no matter what subject it is. Some teachers may even deduct points off your grade because of the spelling errors. In most cases, you can do a spell check on your computer. You can also ask your friend to check your paper for spelling errors. It is unnecessary for obvious misspellings to spoil the overall impression of your paper.

In English or . . . ?

Should you write the first draft (first versions) in English or in your own language? Some students ask whether or not to use their native tongue when they write drafts of papers and then translate their work into the English later. In social science classes, for example, approximately 10 percent of students prefer to take notes in their native language; several class surveys conducted over three years in three schools in Washington, DC, and Virginia provided this evidence. We would advise against this practice. First of all, this is not a wise investment of your time. It takes enormous intellectual effort to translate sentences first from one language into English, and such translations are tiresome and often frustrating. Relying on translation also prohibits the full development of your English language skills. Unless you are going to become a professional translator, try to prepare drafts and take notes in English.

> **⭐ A Useful Tip**
>
> You must have two copies of the assignment. Turn in the original and keep a copy for your files. Always include your name, course title, course number, and the date of the submission on the front page. It will help your professor with the grading.

A Few Words about Recording

It is common to hear from students that they have difficulties writing a paper because they either do not like writing or they have too many thoughts and it is difficult to organize them. In some cases—and again it can be helpful for some students and not so useful to others—you can use tape or digital recording. Indeed, some students prefer to say or dictate their thoughts aloud and then transcribe them into a text. What are the reasons for doing this? Some say it takes less time than to draft a paper. Others suggest that it is easier for them to say things than to write the same things down. Also, if you carry your voice recorder around with you, then you can easily record a thought when it comes to you, no matter what you are doing at the time. Imagine trying to write something down while you are driving a car. That would be too dangerous. Using a voice recording has some clear advantages compared to writing. Moreover, there are several inexpensive voice-converting software applications available today, and this technology is improving rapidly.

How to Display References in Your Paper

We stressed earlier that you should take your required English courses early in your program. In Freshman Composition you will be introduced to and well practiced in writing references. Your comp class should require the purchase and instruct you in the use of a style manual. Keep your manual and learn it well. It will help as you progress into the more advanced courses in your major. Following are some suggestions for citing references:

Example for a book: Indicate author's name, year of publication, book title, city and state of publication, and publisher.

Johnson, J. (2007.) *How to write papers.* Boston: XYZ Publisher.

Example for an article: Include author's name, year of publication, article title, journal name, journal number, month of publication, and article pages.

Robertson, R., and B. Hope, (2006). On using references. *Journal of Modern References 28* (June): 45–50.

Example for a website: include the whole address of the site.
http://references4u.com

Six Rules of Critical Thinking

Today you are a college student—an independent and free person. However, everyone knows that freedom goes hand-in-hand with responsibility. For example, we have to respect and obey both state and federal (national) laws. Moreover, the U.S. Constitution establishes some fundamental principles of life that everyone should follow, no matter how long you have lived here, whether you stay permanently or temporarily. However, in the United States you are free to form your own ideas, ideals, and values. It naturally follows that if you are free to express your ideas, others are free to do the same, even if you dislike their views!

Of course, being tolerant of other people's views is often difficult, and people often argue about the death penalty and abortion, they criticize presidents and local politicians, they have opposing ideas on how to reduce crime and whether or not the rich should help the poor. Sometimes people from other countries have a hard time understanding the constant competition of arguments and may feel confused by such a variety of opinions and beliefs. American culture was developed as a melting pot of ideas, values, and principles of living.

To feel more comfortable within this whirlpool of opinions, one has to develop a strategy to examine, evaluate, and understand events, solve problems, and make decisions on the basis of evidence and reasoning, something that is commonly called critical thinking (Levy 1997). If you understand and know how to apply some major principles of critical thinking to your written work, it will help you better understand evidence, interpret new facts, and defend your own ideas and beliefs.

Critical-Thinking Rule No. 1: Know the Difference between Facts and Opinions

When students solve a math problem, it is expected that he or she will get the same result. This is because, in most cases, there is one, and only one, correct answer for the math problem: 2 × 2 = 4 for all people in every country. However, when you write a paper for sociology, history, psychology, or another social science class, in most cases, there are no "correct" answers. What professors evaluate in your work is the strength of your arguments, or how well your arguments defend your opinions. Why is it important to know the distinction between opinions and facts?

This is a view held by many that descriptions of what we see or hear can never be entirely objective or neutral. People bring into descriptions their personal feelings and values. The words people use not only describe things and events around them, but they can evaluate these things and events. Therefore, in your research papers, unless this is what the professor asks you to do, avoid presenting your value judgments as objective reflections of truth. If you express your opinion, it should be supported by facts that can be verifiable by other people. Facts improve the strength of your argument.

Do not let anyone tell you that you cannot express your opinions. You can express yourself in many ways, and the law protects your right to free speech. But you have to call them your opinions and do not confuse them with facts. For example, if you find data indicating that just 50 percent of eligible voters in the United States actually voted in a presidential election, this is a fact. Why? Because the published data showed how many people voted in the United States at that time. However, when you try to explain this fact, you now express your opinion. You may say, for example, that voter apathy and disappointment in politics caused this relatively low voting turnout. This is your opinion because you do not know why the level was low. You are just guessing. Another person may suggest a different explanation: "The number of voters was low because of people's satisfaction with life. Things were going fine and it did not really matter who is in power. The government played a very small role in people's lives and either candidate would have been fine in office" (Shiraev and Sobel 2006).

Facts are supposed to be neutral. Opinions reflect what you think or feel about the facts. It is a fact that, according to surveys, almost 60 percent of college graduates in the United States plan to move back with their parents for some time, but at the same time almost nine out of ten American parents do not want or would not want their adult children to live with them (Gordon and Shaffer 2004). You are expressing an opinion when you attempt to explain the fact presented in the previous sentence. You may say that young Americans cannot afford to live alone, and therefore they have no choice but move in with their parents. You may also suggest that the ties between parents and children are not as strong as those in many other cultures, and the American parents want their adult children to live separately. These are opinions.

Remember to consider the source of the information. If you have any doubts or concerns about your source, try to find another one. Inaccurate results cannot be proven, or there is a great deal of doubt about their validity. Opinions are always subjective and even if they are based on accurate facts, they reflect the viewpoint of the person who holds the opinion.

✎ A Class Assignment

Consider the following statements. Identify (a) facts and (b) opinions. Explain your choices.

In the United States, homosexuality is considered to be a mental disorder. However, despite many people's objections, this type of sexual behavior is openly discussed in the media.

Homosexuality was considered a disorder prior to 1972. Today, it is not a mental disorder, according to American Psychiatric Association's classification of mental disorders. So the first sentence about homosexuality being a mental disorder is an incorrect statement. The second sentence is a correct fact. Why? Because, indeed, we know through observation that many people have strong negative opinions against homosexuality, and homosexuality is openly discussed in the media.

The average American in the year 2007 made around $40,000 per year.

This is an accurate statement. There are several ways to verify this. For example, the Bureau of Labor Statistics publishes official reports the average annual wages in the country. Source: *www.bls.gov/cew/.*

In the United States, about 30 percent of adults have had at least one divorce in their lives.

This statement reflects evidence obtained through national opinion polls according to which approximately 30 percent of Americans said they have had at least one divorce during their lifetime (2006, Gallup/CNN/USA Today Poll). (Of course, we assume that people tell the truth when responding to surveys.)

Cars are the biggest source of air pollution in the world.

This is an inaccurate statement. Facts show that the biggest source of air pollution today is heating and electricity generation, according to the United Nations and the World Resources Institute, a highly reputable international organization.

Critical-Thinking Rule No. 2: There Are Many Colors in a Rainbow

Many things in life are certain, and we can say *yes* or *no* when we describe them. For example, you passed an exam and got an *A*. It would be untrue to say that you got a *B*.

You arrive at the airport and realize that you are late for your flight and that the plane has already taken off. You missed your plane. You are not on the plane because you are standing at the airport terminal trying to schedule another flight.

If you are born in Korea, your birthplace is not Paris or Lima. These things are obvious, you say. Facts are always facts! Do not be so certain, however. There are many facts people misinterpret every day! We may say, for example, that Mr. Ababaka is unkind and mean because, at times, Mr. Ababaka was unkind to us. Conclusion? He is a mean person. However, do we have evidence that he has never been kind to others? If we do not have such evidence, we can only conclude that Mr. Ababaka was mean in the observable instances.

Most psychological categories and descriptions we assign to people and their behavior do not consider all the factors involved. People describe someone as violent, very happy, indecisive, or undisciplined. Do these descriptions reflect the real situation or tell us a lot about these people? Probably not. What is the level of the person's violence? Is he dangerous or not? How do we define happy? How often does she show indecisiveness?

Critical thinking is about making comparisons. We often say things like, *These two religions are so different,* or *These two ethnic groups are similar to each other.* However, there is nothing that can be perfectly identical or entirely different from other things. Finding the similarities and differences between something is based on the perspectives from which you choose to view them. In this way, most people and events can be seen as both distinct from and, at the same time, similar to other events or people.

> ## ☆ A Useful Tip
>
> Pay attention to whether your paper expresses an opinion or a fact. When you know that you can confirm your statements with available facts, use them, or at least mention their existence. In other cases, do not hesitate to use such phrases as *in my opinion, I think, I believe, it seems to me, according to my views,* and so on.

Think
Critically

When comparing and contrasting something, describe in what ways these things are similar and in what ways they are different. Choose different standpoints from which you will evaluate. Despite what may appear to be an overwhelming number of similarities between two events, always search for and take into account their differences. Conversely, regardless of what may seem to be a total absence of commonalities between two events, search for and take into account their similarities.

Assignment: Despite obvious differences, find and describe similarities between: Republicans and Democrats; New York and Los Angeles; American food and Chinese food; rock music and hip-hop; baseball and basketball; TV and the Internet; public schools and private schools.

Critical-Thinking Rule No. 3: Emotions Should Not Judge Fact!

In the classic TV series *Star Trek*, one of the main characters, Mr. Spock, was half-human, half-alien, and naturally free from any emotions. His behavior was directed by pure logic. He was, of course, a fictional character; all humans experience emotions. A strong emotional commitment to something or somebody is a natural element of human life. However, people's personal likes and dislikes sometimes tell more about the individuals themselves than about the objects under their consideration. Consider the following statements:

"I dislike individuals with liberal views. I think everything they do is an attempt to raise taxes on hard-working Americans."

"I dislike men and women with conservative views and believe that they are narrow-minded and greedy. The only thing they care about is their wallet."

"I love this actor/actress (Wesley Snipes, Tom Cruise, Angelina Jolie) and will buy tickets to see his/her recent premier regardless of what people say about the movie."

"I do not like this actor/actress (Wesley Snipes, Tom Cruise, Angelina Jolie) and will not see his/her recent movie."

"I think that most immigrants to the United States are poor, uneducated, and unskilled individuals who arrive in the country illegally. Therefore, immigration should be restricted."

"I think that most immigrants to the United States are educated and hard-working individuals who arrive in the country in search of a new life. Therefore, immigration should be encouraged and protected."

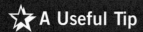

⭐ A Useful Tip

When you work on a paper, keep an open mind to different and, especially, challenging points of view. Do not cling to your emotional judgments, particularly in the face of evidence to the contrary.

Every statement here begins with an evaluation of a particular group. The positive or negative evaluation then results in a suggested action in support of or against the considered people. Our emotions dictate further actions. People often do not have the time or resources to consider all information available to them. Instead, they use emotions to make judgments. We all have a repertoire of such shortcuts that we tend to use automatically, without necessarily considering their accuracy or validity in various life situations.

Thus, we may either like or dislike particular groups of people and individuals because of their nationality, religion, sexual, or political orientation.

Vivid examples, dramatic events, graphic case studies, and personal testimonies, in contrast to statistical information, are likely to exert a disproportionate impact on our judgments. In this way, anecdotes and stories may be more persuasive than factual data. For example, look at any evening news broadcast. Perhaps you are disturbed. You find the local news filled with reports about accidents, theft, robbery, assault, and other violent crime. Persuaded by the intimidating power of the evening news, one may conclude that violent crime is on the rise in this country. In fact, quite the opposite trend has occurred since the middle of the 1990s: The overall rate of violent crimes has gone down since the 1980s. For example, in 1985 there were 497,000 robberies and 580,000 in 1995, but only 417,000 in 2005 (*www.disastercenter.com*).

Another example is that it is very common to hear about how freely American couples live together without getting married. We hear these stories on campus, at home, and in the media. Perhaps many of us have unmarried friends who live together. The question is, how many people in the United States live together without marriage? Half? One-third? Twenty-five percent? In fact, the actual number is much lower. According to surveys only 5 percent of couples in the United States living together are unmarried (Shiraev and Sobel 2006)

One very important way in which our personal views can bias (prejudice) our thinking is when we equate our description of "what is" with our prescription of "what ought to be." This occurs, for instance, whenever we define what is good in terms of what is "typical." Learn to differentiate objective descriptions from subjective prescriptions. Don't make the mistake of equating statistical frequency with moral value. Thus, if most people do something, that does not intrinsically make it right; if most people do not, neither does it make it wrong.

> ## ☆ A Useful Tip
>
> Be empathetic, i.e., try to understand something you do not like from the position of people who disagree with you. Although emotional and vivid events may be very persuasive, they do not necessarily tell us about general tendencies. Make an effort, whenever it is reasonable, to look for statistical information about the event you are examining. When faced with a discrepancy between your beliefs and the facts, resist the natural tendency to assume that your beliefs are right and the facts are wrong.

Critical-Thinking Rule No. 4: Naming Something Is Not Explaining It

In an effort to find an explanation for events or issues, sometimes people commit the following error. Imagine, for instance, that you have to write a paper about aggressive driving on American roads. You seek to explain why many people ignore speed signs, do not use their turn signals, and drive recklessly. You find several newspaper articles on this issue and believe you have found the correct explanation, one that is suggested by the newspaper reporters as well. You establish that the main reason for aggressive driving is people's disregard for the rights of other drivers: Some people do not care about other human beings and are willing to put them in dangerous situations. Be cautious, however. Does this sentence actually explain the nature of aggressive driving? No, it does not because the explanation is redundant. Aggressive driving by definition is, in fact, the disregard for other people's rights on the road. What you set out to do is to explain why some people act carelessly. Perhaps you will conclude that several psychological reasons play a role, such as emotional problems, an inability to stay on schedule, or frustrating events of the day.

Let's take another example. You realize that there are some people in the United States who donate money to charitable organizations. Why do they do this? You may answer that they like to help other people. This answer makes sense, of course, but it does not add anything new to our understanding of generous behavior because it is obvious that a person who does not like to help other people will not donate money to charity. To answer this question from a critical thinking standpoint, you will have to look for several explanations. Some people do charitable work because their religion suggests that they do it. Others give money to charity because they want to get a tax break. Others do it because they were poor themselves and know how nice it is to get support from other people. Some may send money to charity in order to be in line with friends who have already contributed.

⭐ A Useful Tip

Remember: By giving an event a different name, you are not explaining this event. When looking for an explanation to something, ask yourself this question: Does my description add anything to my understanding of this problem? As an example: Your friend tells you that she is always nervous during exams and she does not know why. If you tell her that she has "test anxiety," you probably give a correct label to her problem. However, will it help her to explain why she has test anxiety? A better way to understand the problem is to find out why she feels nervous before and during exams.

As an exercise, find some flaws of reasoning in the following statements:

> "Some people express prejudice against ethnic groups because these people are racists."

> "This man sells his property because he wants to earn some money."

> "The couple is getting a divorce because the husband and wife cannot live together."

A Case in Point

To summarize the materials you have read above, consider another interesting case. Things that appear to us in some way true may not be true in reality. Many people who describe Americans and their lifestyle would say that Americans don't have free time at all, that they are pressured to work all the time. In fact, as sociologists show in their studies, since 1965, an average American has gained an hour more of free time every day. This is happening because, compared to 40 years ago, Americans are working less, marrying later, having fewer children, and retiring earlier. In addition, many people choose to be busy and participate in many activities that their parents didn't (including using the computer, surfing the Internet, playing videogames, and traveling). (Stossel 2006)

Critical-Thinking Rule No. 5: A Link between Two Events Does Not Indicate that One Event Is Causing the Other

Let us begin with an example. It is known that children who are prone to violent behavior tend to watch television programs with violent content more often than non-violent children do. The most obvious explanation that comes to us might be that watching violent television programs may cause violent behavior. However one has to take a more careful look at the problem of violence and television. A different explanation can be offered: What if children with violent tendencies prefer to watch television programs with violent content? Indeed, research indicates that the relationship between aggressive behavior and watching television violence is bi-directional. That is, aggressive children are prone to watch violent TV programs, and television violence, in turn, results in aggressive behavior.

Consider another sociological fact. In the United States and around the world, crime rates in poor neighborhoods are higher than the crime rates in more affluent communities. The simple answer is that poverty causes crime. Is this a wrong assumption? No, it can be a correct one, however, let's look at another option. Crime, in turn, may contribute to poverty as well. Because crime-infested areas do not attract private businesses to invest in them, tourists stay away from these neighborhoods; as a result, new jobs are not created and local residents have fewer opportunities to earn money.

✏ Class Exercise

Consider the links between human creativity and mood disorders. Psychologists have concluded that among creative people, e.g., musicians, poets, and artists, mood disorders are more common than they are in other people (Jamison 1993). What two types of connection can you establish? What causes what? Do mood disorders affect creativity, or does creativity affect mood disorders?

What you see as cause may be seen as effect and vice versa. Many people's answers to the cause-and-effect dilemma are based on their personal views. Does a student have poor English skills because he or she is too shy to talk, or is he or she shy because of a poor English vocabulary? Every possibility might be both a cause and an effect on the other. Remember the chicken-and-egg question: Which came first? Quite often, questions of this type are difficult to answer.

When we judge other people, we have a tendency to explain their behavior in context of their own personality. At the same time, we often minimize (or even ignore) the importance of the particular context or situation. For example, imagine a person you know who does not say hello to you in passing. The person, then, is rude. Or isn't he? Maybe he did not see you, or he was extremely preoccupied with his own thoughts. Maybe you didn't say hello loud enough. If somebody doesn't want to lend you his notes, you consider this person to be inconsiderate. You do not know that maybe this person has already promised to give the notes to somebody else, or maybe is planning to study them at home. American journalists know this tendency of human judgment.

☆ A Useful Tip

A link between events does not prove that there is a one-directional causal relationship between them. If somebody presents two events and shows that they happen at the same time, it does not necessarily follow that event A has caused event B. Although knowing about a link enables us to make predictions about variables, it does not permit us to draw unequivocal conclusions as about the source or direction of causes and effect.

Critical-Thinking Rule No. 6: When You Explain Why Certain Things Happen, Think about Many Causes

Imagine that your friend got involved in a fender-bender (a minor car accident): She bumped into another car near an intersection. When you ask your friend to explain what happened, she says that the girl in a car in front of her suddenly stopped on the yellow light, and as a result of this "sudden" stop your friend did not have enough time to react properly and push the brakes. "So, who caused the accident?" you ask. "The car ahead of me," your friend replies. Did it? When you ask your friend to tell you more about her day, you realize that to begin with, she was at a birthday party the night before and came home late. Because she went to bed very late, she overslept in the morning. Because she was in a hurry to get to school, she jumped into her car and forgot to take her purse, so she had to make a u-turn and go back home, which took her another 20 minutes. Her frustration grew because of the traffic on the main street. To beat the traffic and be at school on time, she decided to take a short-cut. Then she got lost. Because she was desperately late, she started to drive very fast and ignore speed limits. As a result, she got involved in an accident.

Now try to answer the question: What was the cause of the accident? Was it a car that stopped at the intersection? Or was it your friend's decision to stay late at that party? Or was it because she overslept and left her bag in her apartment? Or maybe heavy traffic on the main street was to blame? Now you can predict the direction of this reasoning: From a critical thinking standpoint, all the above circumstances could have contributed to the collision.

Let us use another example. Florida, a state in the southeast part of the United States, has the highest percentage of the population (19 percent) over age 65. On the other hand, Alaska has the lowest percentage of people over 65 (6 percent). Could you explain this trend? Some may quickly suggest that the answer is the climate. Alaska has the harshest climate in the United States, whereas Florida is known for its warm weather. However, weather could be a poor predictor of why American senior citizens choose a particular state to live. Pennsylvania and Rhode Island, two states that come in second and third with almost 16 percent over age 65, have climates quite different from Florida's and severe winters. The answer may be that there is no single answer regarding why some individuals choose a particular place to live. For some people it could be climate (cold or warm), for others it could be low property tax. Some people move closer to their children and grandchildren. Some want to go back to their hometowns.

For Class Discussion

The states with the highest proportion of population under 18 are Utah (33 percent), Alaska (31 percent), and Idaho (29 percent), all three with relatively harsh climates. Can you explain this tendency as climate-related? What other factors may cause a high level of young people in a state?

The top five states with the highest proportion of doctors (more than 300 per 100,000 population) are all in the northeastern United States: Massachusetts, New York, Maryland, Connecticut, and Rhode Island. Do you think doctors like the weather conditions of these regions? What other factors may affect a doctor's decision to live in a particular state?

Take a look at some more examples. What triggers the development of mental disorders? Is it genetic and other biological factors? Unfavorable social conditions? Continuing stress? Persistent abuse? The answer is that all of the above conditions may contribute (Levy 1997). What causes almost one million people to apply for American citizenship every year? Is this motivated by their desire to escape injustice and war in their home countries? Maybe these people are in search of a better life in the United States. Maybe America offers greater educational opportunities for their children. Or maybe this decision is based on a desire to reunite with relatives. Apparently, all the above reasons can be true (Shiraev and Levy 2007). What causes violent behavior in some individuals? Is it the long-term abuse and injustice they suffered, or a short temper that is quick to anger? Apparently both, as the research showed (Tsytsarev and Grodnitzky 1995).

★ A Useful Tip

In attempting to explain why an event occurred, don't limit your search to one cause. Instead, explore multiple plausible causes, all of which may be responsible for producing the effect. When faced with an either/or question, always consider the possibility that the answer might be both.

It is known that wealthier people live longer and are generally healthier than poorer people. Why is this? One obvious reason is that wealthier people can afford more medical care than the less fortunate. However, other factors contribute to this trend. For example, people with higher income smoke less, exercise more, maintain healthy body weight, eat nutritious meals, and face less psychological stress than other groups. (Lewis 2001)

One more case: In 2005, Americans spent more than $1.8 trillion on credit cards. In 1995, they spent $1.3 billion. In 1990, they charged only $796 billion (for recent updates check *www.cardweb.com*). Does it mean that Americans are spending more than they did in the recent past? It may be true. However, one can offer another plausible suggestion that Americans simply have started to use credit cards more often than they did ten years ago. Today, most small businesses will accept your credit card, which was not the case in the previous decades. If it is convenient and people like this payment system, they are more willing to use plastic instead of cash and checks.

For Class Discussion

Try to find multiple causes/ explanations to the following questions:

- In your opinion, why are the divorce rates higher in the United States than they are in Kuwait?
- In your opinion, why are crime rates in American cities higher than those in urban areas?
- In your opinion, why is the American female soccer team among the best in the world, whereas the American men have had poor performance in international soccer championships?
- In your opinion, why is *CSI: Miami* among the most popular television shows in the world?

Detail, Details

What is the appropriate writing style for a formal or informal paper? A paper written informally resembles a conversation and conveys emotions such as joy, frustration, and surprise. It may be sarcastic or humorous. A formal style is more neutral in terms of the emotions conveyed. Formal papers contain no slang; informal papers allow the usage of slang. For example, using formal style, you always describe a person as a man or woman, lady or gentleman, human being or person. Using the informal style, you can address another person as dude, guy, bro, or pal.

Under no circumstances would it be appropriate to use profanity in your reports. According to traditions of higher education, it is always expected that the writer find other acceptable words to describe people's actions and personalities.

No matter what style you choose, refer to yourself as "I," or use the slightly more formal "we." Pay attention to gender-related words as some readers could be sensitive to gender bias in your paper. Remember, there are congressmen and congresswomen; it is appropriate to write "chairwoman" and "spokeswoman." If you do not know how to reflect gender in someone's title, learn how to use gender-neutral words, such as firefighter (both a man and a woman can be a firefighter), cop, officer, chair, and specialist.

You would be surprised how small things can spoil the overall quality of your paper. Therefore, when the paper is finished, check to see if you took care of all the "minor" details that can affect your grade. Be sure to submit a title page with the paper if the professor requires it. If you use references, include the reference list, even though it may contain only a few items. Unless otherwise requested by the professor, always staple the pages of the paper. Leave 2-inch to 2.5-inch margins so that the professor can write comments on them. Use 1.5-line or 2-line spacing. Always have a second copy of your work, and keep it with your class materials. Submit your paper on time (see the box that follows). Organize your time. Revise your paper and let it rest. Use a proofreader if possible.

Think
Critically

The following are some excuses that students still use and almost every college professor has already heard at least several times. Therefore, do not use them because your professor is likely to offer a powerful argument in response:

My computer's hard drive crashed yesterday. My brother (sister, nephew, cousin, dog, cat, etc.) accidentally deleted my file.
Response: Have a copy of your work on a removable diskette or portable storage device.

My printer is out of ink, and my printer's cartridge is out of powder.
Response: Do your printing job at any of the school's printers.

I had two (three, four, etc.) tests this week, so I need an extension. Or: Professor, I was thinking a lot about the assignment and finally realized that I do not quite understand the assignment.
Response: Do your work in advance; you knew about this assignment a long time ago.

I couldn't open my file on the school's computer. May I bring the paper tomorrow?
Response: Try to open the file at least a day before your paper is due. Ask the computer lab staff to help you.

Professor, here is my diskette [waving one], I have just a few final touches to make; let me bring the paper later.
Response: Do not think that you are smarter than your professor and that just seeing the disk will impress him or her. Bring your paper instead.

Avoid Plagiarism

Sometimes you browse the Internet or look through a pile of books in the library and find the perfect material for your report or paper. The site offers almost everything you need: a great introduction, a literature review, solid empirical data, a critical analysis of the data, a spectacular conclusion, and even a bibliography! While contemplating an inevitable *A,* you copy this material from the website (or scan it) and paste into your file. You change the fonts and the design of the report, put your name on the top, and submit it to your professor. What you have done is called **plagiarism,** or intentional use of someone else's ideas as your own. Plagiarism is cheating and can be severely penalized (you can fail the class and be expelled from college). In some cases you can be charged with a violation of copyright laws, and the consequences of this action can be very serious. Remember, you have to submit your own ideas. If you base your report on the ideas of other people, you must include their names and mention their publications. Do not think you can trick your professor by changing the introduction and conclusion, leaving the middle part intact. The paper is still plagiarized. Do not try to substitute 10, 15, 20 words from the original text with your own. It will still be unacceptable. Do not submit one paper to several professors for different classes. Likewise, do not use a paper written by another student and claim that it is yours. Remember, one silly mistake may influence your entire college career. Many colleges subscribe to services that can be used to detect plagiarism, and many professors are computer savvy and can detect plagiarism from their own computers.

> ## ⭐ A Useful Tip
>
> If you want to avoid plagiarism, mention the author whose work you are using as often as seems natural in the paper. There is nothing wrong in promoting other people's ideas and giving them credit for their work. Use quotation marks if you want to cite an entire sentence or two. However, do not make the citations too frequent and too long.

PART 3

Negotiating American Culture

art 1 addressed many of the difficult and confusing technical details that students need to understand to comfortably and successfully arrive in the United States and begin studying. Chapter 3 discussed the concept of acculturation stress and what happens when the culture you bring as an international student interacts with the cultural realities of a new school that exists in a new community, in a new state, in a new country.

Part 2 focused on important skills and strategies to help you understand what is expected of you in the classroom and in your coursework. Most of the issues in Parts 1 and 2 relate to both significant and subtle institutional differences that you will immediately encounter upon arrival and as you begin to negotiate the college and community in which you have selected to study and live. Not knowing about these issues can cause confusion and make adjusting to life in your new setting difficult.

It is important to understand and be prepared to deal with a new setting that will be different from and may not operate the way you are used to and the way you like best. Your goal will be to develop ways in which you can recognize and adapt to new situations you may or may not fully understand.

Part 3 discusses aspects of the culture in the United States that will help you *begin* to understand the sometimes confusing and frequently misunderstood concept of American culture.

CHAPTER 7

American Culture

> **W**e live in an age of fateful challenges. As a nation and a people, we are [being tested]. Each of us can look forward to many years of uncertainty and peril—but also of work and hope. The revolutionary forces shaking the earth have converged, presenting us with hard choices, with a need for action, for ideas, for concerted and sustained commitment as a nation and as individual citizens. We are challenged by the revolution of hope in continents long captive by stagnation and despair. We are challenged by the revolution of science and technology bringing new boons and new dangers to humanity. We are challenged by their revolution in international relationships. Nation has begun to work with nation to solve mankind's problems. New international bodies are exploring uncharted paths of world cooperation and interests of worldwide peace, justice, and freedom.

President John F. Kennedy addressed these words to American citizens in 1963. Do Americans face different challenges today? Have starvation and despair ceased to exist? Have Americans stopped their pursuit of equality, wider opportunities, and greater dignity for their diverse nation? Can modern technologies be a threat to democracy and international peace? Have people stopped worrying about international security? Do we still need new actions and new ideas? America of the 1960s is certainly different from the country of today. However, many remarkable features of American culture, people's hopes, dreams, worries, customs, and habits remain the same. In some ways, Americans resemble citizens of other countries—they want to live in peace, go to school and work, have a decent home, and have good friends. In other ways, however, Americans are different. Let's try to understand them better.

It is very complicated to begin a dialogue about culture in the United States. At first, one might think that there isn't any clear culture and that the United States is a society of fragmented and competing groups of people. This is not the case.

The United States has a heterogeneous population, which means it is made up of many different groups that make it diverse and multicultural. Americans have a cultural identity that has many dimensions and is described as **pluralistic**—meaning "people of different races, religions, and political beliefs living together peacefully in the same society." This is particularly true in urban areas, but it is becoming more of a reality in all parts of the country.

Defining Culture

The idea of culture can be divided into six aspects according to Stern (1992) and Maley (1993):

- **Places.** This has to do with geography: local and regional variation.
- **History**. The objective set of facts and events that shaped a region and the perceptions and beliefs people have about their own history.
- **Individual persons**. How people live and what they think, do, and value.
- **People in society**. The way in which a society functions and how economic, professional, age, sex, gender, and religious groups interact in it.
- **Institutions**. The influence of the democratic system of government and how the bureaucracy, education, social welfare, law, and the media interact.
- **Art, music, literature, sports, and other major achievements**.

Places

In Chapter 1, you were advised to carefully select the school you plan to attend based on your program of study and the area of the country in which you are interested. There is a great deal of geographic variation in the United States, and that variation can potentially have an immense impact on the quality of your stay. You should fully understand not only the geography of the area in which you plan to study, but also any cultural characteristics of that area. The conterminous states—those states that share a border with another state, thus forming the major body of the United States—can be divided into regions that reflect common characteristics; however, each state has its own personality and charm. Hawaii and Alaska are strongly influenced by their unique and beautiful geography and by their detachment from the conterminous states. Canada separates Alaska from the mainland, and Hawaii is composed of five islands in the Pacific Ocean.

Region	States in the Region	Regional Character
New England	Connecticut, Maine, Massachusetts, New Hampshire, Rhode Island, Vermont	Rocky wooded mountain and valley areas, picturesque seaports, and rocky coastlines with a great deal of natural beauty. Mild summer, fall, and spring seasons with cold winters.
Middle Atlantic	Delaware, Maryland, New Jersey, New York, Pennsylvania, Virginia, West Virginia, Washington, DC	Rolling wooded areas and low to medium mountain ranges. Lush, green valleys with moderate vegetation. Very good farmland. Highly developed coastal areas. Cold winters and hot summers with mild fall and spring seasons.
The South	Alabama, Arkansas, Florida, Georgia, Kentucky, Louisiana, Mississippi, North Carolina, South Carolina, Tennessee	Rolling, wooded areas with low to medium mountain areas. Much more vegetation than in the Middle Atlantic, and it is sub-tropic to tropic. Many rivers and lakes run through the South. Farming is good. Mild winter, fall, and spring seasons, with very hot and humid summers.
The Plains	Kansas, Nebraska, North Dakota, South Dakota	Very large areas of flat grassy land in Kansas and Nebraska, more rocky and mountainous in the Dakotas. This area tends to be dry and has very harsh winters, with mild spring, fall, and summer seasons. Farming and raising livestock are good in this region.
The Midwest	Illinois, Indiana, Iowa, Michigan, Minnesota, Missouri, Ohio, Wisconsin	This region is characterized by the Great Lakes and the other lakes and rivers that run throughout the region, including the Mississippi River. This region has mountains and wooded areas, as well as rolling flatlands, and is excellent for farming and livestock. Mild summer, fall, and spring seasons, and long, cold winters.
The Southwest	Arizona, Colorado, Nevada, New Mexico, Oklahoma, Southern California, Texas, Utah	These states all have relatively dry climates that are either desert-like or extremely mountainous. The desert areas are very hot in the summer season with mild winter, fall, and spring seasons. The northern areas of Arizona, New Mexico, Colorado, and Utah can have severe winters, with heavy snowfall. This region has breathtaking canyon regions.
The Northwest	Idaho, Montana, Northern California, Washington, Wyoming	Great mountainous, wooded areas with rocky coastlines are characteristic of this region. This region is full of natural beauty and is not highly populated. Mild summer, fall, and spring seasons with relatively wet winters.

Source: America the Beautiful, Brompton Book Co., 1988.

History: Democratic Government

We could not possibly cover the details of the history of the development of the United States in this text. However, it is important to note some significant historical issues that relate to the country's culture. Like all countries in the world, the culture of this country has been strongly influenced by its historic developments. Even though the United States is a relatively young country compared to others, it has had a rich history and has risen in a relatively short time to be a powerful nation.

From the settlement of Jamestown, Virginia, in 1620 to the present, people have been coming to this country to begin a new life in which they are in control of their personal lives. This is reflected in the documents that serve as the basis of democracy in the United States: The Declaration of Independence and the Constitution.

In 1776, the Declaration of Independence gave notice to the ruling colonial government from Great Britain that "these united colonies [America] are, and of right ought to be, free and independent states." Thomas Jefferson, the principle author of the document, stated that:

> ## ☆ A Useful Tip
>
> Most states have a website that provides information and statistics. Try *www.state.*[postal abbreviation].*us.*
>
> Each state has a postal abbreviation of two characters: **CA** stands for California, **NY** for New York, **OR** for Oregon, **TX** for Texas, **NC** for North Carolina, and so on. For example, for California you would type *www.state.ca.us* and for Virginia you would type *http://www.state.va.us*

> We hold these truths to be self-evident, that all men are created equal, that they are endowed by their Creator with certain unalienable rights, that among these are life, liberty, and the pursuit of happiness. That to secure these rights, governments are instituted among men, deriving their powers from the consent of the governed. That whenever any form of government becomes destructive to these ends, it is the right of the people to alter or abolish it, and to institute new government, laying its foundation on such principles and organizing its powers on such principles, and organizing its powers in such forms as to them shall seem most likely to effect their safety and happiness.

The U.S. Constitution was approved by the 13 original colonies in 1789. This document became the blueprint of the U.S. government and established the initial laws of the land. The Constitution is composed of Articles I–VIII (one through eight), which established the structure of the democratic form of government, ensuring a balance of power among the executive, judicial, and legislative units. This is called separation of powers, designed to prevent the executive from acting as if he were a king.

The **executive branch** is represented by the President, the Vice President, and the Cabinet, which consists of the heads of the executive departments, and the support staff that help the President run his end of the government. (We are using the masculine pronouns *he* and *his* to refer to the President because there has not yet been a woman President, although someday there might be.) The Executive branch is often referred to as The White House in the media; however, the executive branch has offices in many other places. The President and his family live in The White House, which has offices for the President and his large staff.

The main function of the executive branch is to provide leadership for the federal government and to represent the United States around the world. The President's role of running the government is in direct relation to the other branches of government. The President is not all powerful. Both the judicial and the legislative branches temper his power. In addition, he must ultimately answer to the people.

The **legislative branch** of the government is composed of the House of Representatives and the Senate. The Senate and the House make up what is referred to as the **Congress.** The legislative branch has always had "the power of the purse." The control of the budget of the U.S. government is a powerful check on the executive branch. The Senate consists of 100 members: two senators from each state who serve six-year terms. Currently the House consists of 435 voting members that represent the states based on the size of the population, and each member serves two-year terms. The House and the Senate work on originating bills that set policy and designate money for the operation of the federal government; they also decide how many of the governmental agencies should operate. Bills are proposed laws that must be approved by a majority of the House and the Senate and are ultimately signed into law by the President. The President's check on the legislative branch is that he has the power to sign or veto (reject) a bill from Congress. Congress creates laws; the President signs them into law; and the judicial branch of the government interprets and makes rulings based on law.

The **judicial branch** of the government is represented by the federal court system, which is composed of the Supreme Court and the circuit and the district court systems. The circuit court system and the district court system handle most of the federal cases—those that affect citizens in all states. The Supreme Court makes final interpretations of law, a sort of guardian of the Constitution.

The Constitution also has XXVII (27) amendments that add to the content of the original articles. The first ten amendments are known as the Bill of Rights and were approved in order to protect individual freedom from the tyranny of government. The constitution has held up well for more than 200

Rights Enumerated in the Bill of Rights[*]

First Amendment

- Right to freedom of religion, speech, and press.
- Right to assemble peaceably, and to petition the government for a redress of grievances.

Second Amendment

- Right to keep and bear arms in common defense.

Third Amendment

- Right not to have soldiers living in one's home in peacetime without the consent of the owner, nor in time of war except as prescribed by law.

Fourth Amendment

- Right to be secure against "unreasonable searches and seizures."

Fifth Amendment

- Right, in general, not to be held to answer criminal charges, except upon indictment by a grand jury.
- Right not to be charged more than once for the same crime.
- Right not to be compelled to be a witness against oneself in a criminal case.
- Right not to be deprived of life, liberty, or property without due process of law.
- Right to just compensation for private property taken for public use.

Sixth Amendment

- In criminal prosecution, right to a speedy and public trial by an impartial jury, to be informed of the charges, to be confronted with witnesses, to have a compulsory process for calling witnesses in defense of the accused, and to have legal counsel.

Seventh Amendment

- Right to a jury trial in suits at common law involving more than $20.

Eighth Amendment

- Right not to have excessive bail required, nor excessive fines imposed, nor cruel and unusual punishments inflicted.

Ninth Amendment

- Enumeration of certain rights in the Constitution shall not be construed to deny or disparage others retained by the people.

Tenth Amendment

- The powers not delegated to the United States by the Constitution, nor prohibited by it to the States, are reserved to the States, respectively, or to the people.

---

[*] *Our American Government*, U.S. Government Printing Office. Washington, DC, 1993, pp. 3–4.

years because it has carefully been amended to meet the changes in the country's development. (For more detailed information about the U.S. government, go to *http://thomas.loc.gov.*)

One of the fundamental principles of the United States that affects the culture is the importance of the freedom of the individual person. The **Founding Fathers** were careful to make this clear from the start of the country. The idea of individual freedom is strongly represented in the Declaration of Independence and the U.S. Constitution, especially in the Bill of Rights.

Throughout the history of the United States, the Supreme Court has diligently protected the concept of individual freedom and continues to do so to this day. The protections provided within the Constitution form the backbone of what liberty and freedom mean to the people of the United States, and are what attract people to this country in great numbers. These freedoms are not the freedom to do anything you please: You cannot infringe upon the rights of others or put others in danger, but you can live knowing that there are protections in place that keep the government from treating you unjustly.

Many of the changes to the Constitution have been to extend freedom and protection to groups that were not included in the initial experiment of democracy. Over time, all of the legal rights of the Constitution have been given to women and minority groups, giving equal status to all the people of the United States, regardless of race, gender, or religious beliefs. This legal equality has been hard earned, often by protest or violence. In practice, there are still many lingering inequalities in how women and minorities are treated, but our culture is moving in a corrective direction (see Chapters 8 and 9).

Individual Persons

The individual has always been idolized in our culture. Strong individual efforts have been captured in our early folktales and glorified in our interpretations of history and in literature. Men like Lewis and Clark, Daniel Boone, and Davy Crockett, who helped the westward settlement of the country, are characterized in American folklore as rugged adventurers. The accomplishments of famous cowboys like William "Buffalo Bill" Cody, Wyatt Earp, "Doc" Holiday, Judge Roy Bean, William "Bat" Masterson, Wild Bill Hickok, and Pat Garrett have been captured in romantic western tales. Calamity Jane and Annie Oakly also captured the spirit of the Wild West. Harriet Tubman was a leader for the Underground Railroad (the path to the North and freedom for slaves).

Native Americans, who have sometimes been cast negatively, had their heroes as well. Geronimo, Sitting Bull, Crazy Horse, and Black Elk were leaders who witnessed the devastation of their own cultures as a result of the westward expansion of the United States. The history of Native Americans is long and rich. Today their voices are contributing productively to the current dialogue of race and ethnicity in our culture.

American public opinion is traditionally sensitive to such issues as the image of "underdog," which is often attached to people and groups struggling for their independence. Many people in the United States have had an almost equal fascination with the outlaw. Famous outlaws like Butch Cassidy and the Sundance Kid, Clay Allison, Black Bart, William "Billy the Kid" Bonney, the Dalton Brothers, John Wesley Harden, and Jesse James were all either thieves or murderers who have been romanticized in print and film. As in nearly all countries in the world, the attention of the American public has shifted to movie stars, athletes, and other celebrities who frequently become famous not only by what they do but because of the attention paid to them by the media.

The influence of the hero and anti-hero runs throughout our history and is reflected in the culture that we experience today. The values reflected by the powerful, adventurous, and uncompromising individual have continuously been reborn or reinvented in our culture. From the early adventurers (the cowboys and Native Americans) to the gangsters of the 1930s and '40s, to the rebellious youth of the 1950s, the civil rights protesters of the 1960s, the anti-Vietnam War demonstrators of the 1970s, and to the politicians, entertainers, movie stars, and entrepreneurs of the past 20 years—they all in some way can be identified as well-known, popular individuals.

People in Society

Americans are not always viewed positively around the world. Sometimes when traveling abroad, they deserve and reaffirm negative stereotypes as a result of their behavior, although there are times they don't deserve labels. They particularly may not deserve the stereotypes that are the result of what one sees in the media. Americans as portrayed in movies are quite different from "real" Americans.

As mentioned in Chapter 1, Americans are divided about how they feel about our military involvement in the Middle East. No matter how an individual American feels about the war in Iraq, that involvement has affected how the rest of the world responds to America as a nation, and as individuals when traveling abroad. Choices made by the government reflect on the citizens of the United States because we elect our government leaders in a free election so that they represent our interests when they make decisions in running the country.

Democracy is inseparable from voting. In simple terms, voting is just a sequence of human actions. At a certain time of the day—morning, afternoon, or evening—an individual goes to a polling place that is near his or her home. Polling places are usually a local school, city hall, library, or other community building. When a voter arrives at the polling place, he or she typically waits in lines for a few minutes and then waits for his or her name to be checked off the list of registered voters. Then the voter goes inside a voting booth or to a small voting station where no one else can see who the voter is voting for. Voting takes place by pushing a button, marking a ballot, or punching a hole through a ballot.

Although the procedures appear simple and the voting itself takes only a few minutes, the votes that represent the opinions of voters transform democratic society in many ways. The ability to vote in the United States has long been considered a fundamental right, a basic freedom, and an expression of being a responsible citizen.

The United States is often considered the land of opportunity. It is viewed as a place where someone can begin with relatively little, and—through hard work, ingenuity, and dedication—rise to riches. This has been true for some people, but for most people it is a life of "ups and downs," just like everywhere else, and sometimes people do not win the big jack-pot in the end (or even a small one). The United States of America is a very diverse country in terms of socio-economic conditions of its citizens. Historically, it is among the top five countries in terms of average amount of goods and services per person, called GPA. The World Bank estimates this number for the United States at $44,000; compare this to the GPA of China at $8,000 and $12,000 for Russia. Some Americans own factories, oil refineries, television networks, publishing companies, and sports teams. In the United States, there are more than 300 billionaires. Some 23 million Americans own small businesses—print shops, bakeries, dry cleaners, farms, and taxis. Two-thirds of Americans have investments in businesses and banks that provide large incomes. Most Americans, though, work for salaries and wages (Shiraev and Sobel 2006).

For the most part, the United States is a country of hard-working people; both rich and poor. A large part of the population is the middle class. It is the breadth and depth of the middle class that make this country so productive.

> # Think
> ## Critically
>
> What is your view of the people from the United States? What stereotypes or generalizations have you made about who these people are? What is behind those impressions? Make a list of the (a) positive and (b) negative characteristics of the people of the United States and discuss the source of these impressions.

However, for a wealthy nation (in terms of resources) that gives to the rest of the world, it has a great deal of poverty. Many international students are surprised when they first arrive in the United States and see poor people and some who are living on the streets. It is part of the culture to help get the homeless into a position that they can help themselves when possible. Help is offered through religious and community groups, and through government social programs.

The family is still the primary unit of the culture, and it is highly valued, even though every family may not look or behave in the same ways. There are people in the U.S. who are religious, as well as those who are not, and they all get along for the most part. Those that are religious can usually find a variety of churches, mosques, temples, and synagogues from which to choose. For those who aren't religious, there is a separation of church and state (in the U.S. Constitution) that frees people from having any religion imposed on them.

> ## Think Critically
>
> What is the "American Dream," and what does "keeping up with the Jones's" mean? When you find definitions and explanations for these two terms, try to illustrate them with some examples.

Institutions

U.S. society is made up of individuals, families, communities, and other institutions that create the fabric of its culture. Education, religion, local, state, and the federal government are examples of such institutions. The media, the military, and corporate enterprises are other examples. Institutions have a powerful influence in this country. From the outside, it may look as if the United States is all about its institutions and about how it can make them bigger, better, and more complex. This might seem to be inconsistent with the country's underlying emphasis on the individual, but institutions actually serve as a frame for American individual icons.

You shouldn't form an impression that American heroes are celebrities and villains. We have always had many institutional heroes. For example, the presidential families of Franklin and Eleanor Roosevelt and John and Jacqueline Kennedy were cultural icons in politics that extended to other aspects of society. Military leaders like Ulysses S. Grant, Dwight David Eisenhower, and Colin Powell are a few of the many institutional leaders whose accomplishments carried them into political leadership. Billy Graham, Pat Robertson, Pat Buchanan, and Jerry Falwell have been dominant voices in organized religion. Dr. Martin Luther King, Jr., was the spokesman for the civil rights movement of the 1960s, and Jesse Jackson has continued to carry the civil rights torch ignited by Dr. King. Albert Sloan, J. Paul Getty, Donald Trump, and Bill Gates are representative of business as an institution, and Barbara Walters, Oprah Winfrey, and Walter Cronkite have been personalities for the media. These people, and many others too numerous to mention, sometimes act as role models with whom other people can align themselves when they speak for their representative institutions.

As mentioned earlier, the U.S. is undeniably a capitalistic country. The institutional structure of the United States is complex and well integrated with the market economy. More and more we are seeing corporate alignment with existing institutions. In education, the influence comes in many forms: from advertising in public schools, colleges, and universities to companies influencing research in some universities.

In professional sports, it is clear whose support any given team receives. Watch any event and you will see the high profile of corporations. Many professional sports and arts facilities are named after their corporate sponsors. For example, in 1999 the Washington Redskins football team reached an agreement on a 27-year, $200 million deal with Federal Express, the overnight package delivery service, for the naming rights to the team's stadium. This means that until 2027 the stadium will be renamed FedEx Field. These types of contributions by corporations might be seen as intrusions; however, no one else is standing in line—particularly the government—to offset the billions of dollars contributed by corporate sponsors.

 A Homework Assignment

Watch fifteen-minute segments of at least three different kinds of sports events. Takes notes on the number of corporate advertisements and the ways in which they were presented. Bring your notes to class for discussion. Generally, over the weekend is a good time to see sports programming (baseball from April through October; football from September to January, basketball from November to June; ice Hockey from October to May).

Art, Music, Literature, Sports, and Other Major Achievements

The culture of a country is very often captured in its art, music, literature, and scientific achievements, and, to some extent, by the other ways in which it entertains itself. Today, the people who are successful in providing entertainment in our society have been socially elevated by those of us who are entertained. Movie stars, athletes, musicians, television personalities, comedians, and supermodels are treated in many ways as a sort of royalty. Beyonce, Angelina Jolie, Brad Pitt, Snoop Dog, Tiger Woods, LeBron James, Jennifer Lopez, Chris Rock, and the latest American Idol are ushered in and out wherever they go as if they were heads of states. Their talent has afforded them wealth and privileges in our culture, and our children, for better or for worse, see them as role models. Chapter 10 covers the media and will develop this idea further.

The United States offers a rich variety of arts, and many styles recognized today internationally have roots here. Music forms like jazz, blues, soul, rhythm-and-blues (R & B), disco, rock 'n' roll, country, and rap are firmly rooted in our culture. The United States has much to offer in the arts, some of which pushes the edge, some of which is conventional, and most of which shows a mastery of genre. The United States has also invented baseball and basketball.

The chart on page 139 categorizes several artistic areas and lists some of the representative artists. Do you recognize any of these names? Try entering some of these names into a search engine to find samples of their work.

Campus Culture

Many of these artists were in some way part of or supported by institutions of higher education. In many communities, the college or university is the primary provider of cultural activities. Become aware of the activities on your campus, and make the effort to experience them. Studying is very important, but it is the other things that colleges and universities provide that many people later say were the most influential on them as a person.

Most institutions will charge you an activities fee. This is generally a required fee that is used to enrich the cultural and social activity of the campus. Also, many institutions provide social and orientation events for new students, and some provide social events specifically for international students. You may initially feel very alone when you arrive in the United States; however, you must be aware that there are three groups on most campuses in which you will automatically belong.

Artistic Area	Selected Contributors
Writers, 19th Century	Ambrose Bierce, Ralph Waldo Emerson, Nathaniel Hawthorne, Washington Irving, Henry James, Herman Melville, Edgar Allen Poe, Harriet Beecher Stowe, Henry David Thoreau, Mark Twain (Samuel Clemens)
Writers, First Half of the 20th Century	Sherwood Anderson, James Baldwin, Kay Boyle, Willa Cather, John Dos Pasos, Ralph Ellison, William Falkner, F. Scott Fitzgerald, Ernest Hemingway, Sinclair Lewis, Katherine Anne Porter, John Steinbeck, James Thurber, Eudora Welty
Writers, Second Half of the 20th Century	John Barth, Donald Barthelme, Ann Beattie, Saul Bellow, T. Coraghessan Boyle, John Casey, John Cheever, Tom Clancy, Eldridge Cleaver, John Grisham, John Irving, Erica Jong, Stephen King, Bernard Malamud, Toni Morrison, Joyce Carol Oates, Flannery O'Connor, Anne Rice, Tom Robbins, William Styron, Amy Tan, John Updike, Kurt Vonnegut, Alice Walker
Playwrights	Christopher Durang, Richard Greenberg, Lillian Hellman, Beth Henley, William Inge, George Kaufman, David Mamet, Arthur Miller, Eugene O'Neill, Neil Simon, Wendy Wasserstien, Andrew Lloyd Webber, Thornton Wilder, Tennessee Williams
Poets	Maya Angelou, Elizabeth Bishop, Robert Bly, Gwendolyn Brooks, James Dickey, Emily Dickinson, Lawrence Ferlinghetti, Allen Ginsberg, Robert Hayden, Langston Hughes, Phillip Leviene, James Merril, Margie Piercy, Sylvia Plath, Adrienne Rich, Anne Sexton, Walt Whitman, Richard Wilber, C. K. Williams, James Wright
Artists	Mary Cassatt, John Stewart Singleton Copley, Georgia O'Keefe, Norman Rockwell, Gilbert Stuart, Andy Warhol, James McNeill Whistler
Photographers	Berenice Abbott, Ansel Adams, Margaret Bourke-White, Dorothea Lange, Anne Leibovitz
Sculptors	Alexander Calder, Daniel Chester French, Malvina Hoffman, Anna Hyatt Huntington, Helen Farnsworth Mears, Louise Nevelson, Isamu Noguchi, Gertrude Vanderbilt Whitney
Architects	Henry Richardson, Louis Sullivan, Frank Lloyd Wright
Dancers	Paula Abdul, Fred Astaire, Josephine Baker, Isadora Duncan, Katherine Dunham, Suzanne Farrell, Martha Graham, Gregory Hines, Janet Jackson, Michael Jackson, Gene Kelly, Pearl Primus, Ginger Rogers, Helen Tamiris
Composers	Laurie Anderson, Amy Beach, Carrie Jacobs Bond, Aaron Copland, George Crumb, Elsa Maxwell, Meredith Monk, John Phillip Sousa, Kay Thompson, Francis Thorne, Mary Lou Williams, Frank Zappa

One of those is formed by the other incoming international students. You will more than likely come in with a **cohort** of young men and women from all over the world. You will all experience similar issues and, despite the diversity of the group, you will quickly identify with some of the other members.

Another group consists of the existing international students who are at various stages of cultural adjustment. These students can be very helpful for your orientation and for mentoring you as a new international student. Don't be afraid to ask them questions. Their answers may be the most valuable ones you can get since they have been through the same experiences.

You will also identify with students from the United States who have lived or studied in other countries themselves. They have been through the process of adjusting to another culture and readjusting to their own culture. Many of these students are very comfortable with international students, and some may have lived in your country. Often these students belong to campus groups called Global Nomads. Information about Global Nomads can be found at *http://globalnomads.association.com/*.

Colleges and universities are, at minimum, like communities, and some of the larger universities are like small towns. They have their own character and culture, and there is a wide spectrum of activities from which to choose.

Many institutions, for example, take great pride in their athletic programs. It is up to you to take advantage of this and go to a sports event to cheer your team on. There is nothing like the energy of a stadium or coliseum full of cheering people. Catch a play at the campus theater or a concert by the campus orchestra. If you feel that you are talented in a particular area, take that talent to the appropriate department and let it be developed. International students have made great contributions in the intellectual and cultural life of college campuses in the United States. Don't miss out!

CHAPTER **8**

Gender Roles in the United States

When the sociology professor asked the students to express their opinion about the reasons for a high divorce rate in and among American families, Sonny quickly raised his hand. When he was called, he said that—in his view—most of the problems in the American family take place because women have too much power. "Freedom of action and individualism are poor substitutions for responsibility, respect, and sense of duty," he added. He also said that in America, too many women are preoccupied with their own personal issues, such as equality, and they forget about their responsibilities as mothers and daughters.

Sonny did not expect his words would cause such criticism from so many students in the class. They angrily replied that for many years equality and freedom have been the most important issues for which American women have been struggling. One student even called Sonny's opinion "sexist," and another suggested that he think before expressing such views in class. Sonny left the classroom confused. After all, he did almost exactly what the professor had asked—he had simply tried to express his opinion. He went to the professor's office to ask for his advice. What bothered Sonny was that he believed his liberty to speak was sacred in America.

"Do not be afraid," commented the professor. "Nobody should limit your right to speak. However, you have to understand that people also have the right to criticize your ideas! We touched on a very delicate issue: gender roles. Very often how you express your ideas is as important as what you say. Try to learn more about issues related to equality between men and women, gender bias, and sex discrimination. These views can be quite different from those accepted in your home country, and that is okay. I will not say you should embrace what most Americans consider to be right. I simply want you to learn more about gender roles here. In fact, your goal is to learn, correct?"

This chapter discusses some of the essential elements of gender and gender roles in the United States. Basic information about the societal relationships between men and women, major social policies related to women, and especially those guiding principles that promote equality between the sexes will be presented.

Some Demographics

As in most countries in the world, in all categories of the U.S. adult population, there are more women than men (See Table 8.1). Some social scientists suggest that women are expected to live longer than men because of genetic and other biological factors.

TABLE 8.1. Overall Number of Women and Men in the United States, in Millions, Estimated

Gender	Overall	Age 20–44	Age 45–64	Age 65–84
Women	157,000,000	52,000,000	42,000,000	19,000,000
Men	152,000,000	53,000,000	40,000,000	15,000,000

Source: U.S. Census Bureau, 2007.

However, most experts refer to other, non-biological reasons that affect higher death rates among men. For example, men traditionally occupy more dangerous and risk-related jobs, such as those in public safety and the armed forces. Also, there are more fatal car accidents involving men than women, and men are more likely to be engaged in aggressive, reckless, and risk-taking behavior (Wharton 2004). In addition, psychologists explain that women are better able to cope with stress and frustration than men are, and this may also explain why the life expectancy for women is higher (Shiraev and Levy 2007).

TABLE 8.2. Number of Men and Women over 65 and 85 Years of Age in 2010, Estimated

Gender	Age 65–84	Age 85 and Over
Women	19,051,000	4,182,000
Men	15,069,000	1, 942,000

Source: U.S. Census Bureau, 2007.

According to 2007 U.S. Bureau of Census data, approximately 25 percent of adult Americans (over age 18) are not married. About one-third of married couples live without children (the couple either does not have children or they have children elsewhere who have already left the family). Approximately one-quarter of American adults live with their children. In the 2000s, approximately 2.4 million marriages took place in the United States every year, but there were also about 1.2 million divorces (dissolution of marriages) per year (U.S. Department of Health and Human Services 2007).

On average, American women in the 2000s had two children. This statistic varies, however, among different groups. For example, African-American women have approximately 2.5 children, and Hispanic women (of South American and Central American origin) have approximately 3 children per person. Some research shows on the national level that the higher the income and educational level of a woman, the fewer children she has (Macionis 2005).

For many years in the United States, men provided a greater percentage of the income to the family than women. This trend began to change after the 1950s. However, there is still a significant gap between men and women in terms of their earnings (see Table 8.3).

TABLE 8.3. Median Income of Men and Women in the United States

Category	Median Income per Year Age Group: Over Age 15, Working Full-Time
Women	$31,223
Men	$40,798

Source: U.S. Census Bureau, 2007.

There can be several explanations why the earnings gap between men and women still exists. For example, more women than men have part-time jobs or occupy temporary and low-paying positions. This is primarily because they have small children and therefore cannot or do not want to be employed full-time. Also, as shown in Table 8.4, more men than women have earned doctoral degrees. Typically, a higher academic degree produces a higher income. The lower the degree, the lower the salary, generally speaking. There is also evidence that men receive more money than women to do the same job. In addition, there are unwritten practices that have favored men over women in terms of salary and consideration for promotion to higher-paying jobs. This hidden discrimination against women has caused the U.S. government to begin taking steps to guarantee women equal protection under the law. In most employment cases today, the relationship between the employer and employee are regulated by special rules supported by federal and state laws.

TABLE 8.4. Educational Attainment of Persons 15 Years and Over

Gender	Bachelor's Degree	Master's Degree	Doctorate Degree
Women	14,441,000	5,326,000	654,000
Men	15,217,000	5,200,000	1,407,000

Source: U.S. Census Bureau, 2007.

Sex, Gender, and Equality

We should briefly explain the difference between the words *sex* and *gender* in the way they are understood today in the United States. *Sex* refers to the biological and anatomical differences between males and females. A newborn baby can be identified by the child's sex as being either male or female. *Gender* refers to socially constructed differences between men and women based on societal norms and values. Newborn babies acquire these roles and become boys and girls and then men and women.

Probably the most important social and political issue in the relationship between men and women in the United States is equality between sexes. There is formal equality, in terms of legal rights, and there is practical equality. In many countries, the law guarantees equal opportunity and many other types of equality for men and women. However, in practice, men still have more power, more access to resources, and, therefore, better opportunities than women.

Over time, some general divisions of labor have occurred between the sexes. In the United States, more men work in public and professional spheres than do women. There are significantly fewer men in such areas as child education, child rearing, and homemaking, although being a "stay at home dad" is on the rise. For example, according to the U.S. Department of Labor (2006), only 9 percent of registered nurses in the United States are men. Social roles, stereotypes, and expectations continue to influence the developmental process of both men and women.

American Public Views on Gender Equality

Americans had to go a long way before their attitudes on equality between the sexes began to change. Egalitarian attitudes—those views that support equality between men and women—did not suddenly occur in opinion polls. In 1936, for example, only 36 percent of Americans believed that there should be more women in politics. Fewer than a one-third of Americans in the 1930s favored a possible appointment of a woman to the Cabinet (when Franklin D. Roosevelt appointed Frances Perkins to the Cabinet). Even in the late 1960s, only half of Americans supported the idea of a woman candidate for president (Erskine 1971).

The situation has changed dramatically since the beginning of the 1970s. A 1984 Gallup Poll found that nearly nine out of ten Americans would vote for a woman candidate for mayor, governor, or for a seat in Congress (Gallup 1985). This trend has continued through the 1990s and is present today. Most surveys on gender equality and perception of women show that from 70 to 80 percent of Americans would vote for a woman presidential candidate (Shiraev and Sobel 2006).

✎ A Class Exercise

What is your view on gender roles? Are you egalitarian or traditional in your views? Indicate your opinion regarding these statements by circling the answer that best represents your feelings. The numbers in parentheses indicate the number of points you get for each answer.

1. If a couple lives together, who should do most of the house work, like cleaning, cooking, decorating, and washing?

   Mostly she (2) Both equally (1) Mostly he (0)

   Explain your decision _____

   _____

2. If a couple lives together, who should have more freedom of action: she or he?

   Mostly he (2) Both equally (1) Mostly she (0)

   Explain your decision _____

   _____

3. If a couple can afford two cars, a new model and a 1987 model, and both work just five miles from home, who should drive the newer car?

   Mostly he (2) Both equally (1) Mostly she (0)

   Explain your decision _____

   _____

4. If a couple's child gets sick with a cold, and one of the working parents—who are equally busy—should pick up their sick child from school, who should do it?

   She (2) Hard to tell (1) He (0)

   Explain your decision _____

   _____

5. The family budget should be generally under control of:

   Husband (2) Both spouses equally (1) Wife (0)

   Explain your decision _____

   _____

Add your scores. If your score is between **8 and 10,** your attitudes are traditional; between **0 and 2,** your attitudes are feminist; between **3 and 7,** your attitudes are egalitarian.

Men, Women, and Attitudes

How different are men and women in terms of their views on particular social issues? Historically, women in the United States have been and are more opposed than men to the use of force. Women have also been more supportive of gun control and opposed to capital punishment. Women have shown greater support for school prayer, social help for the needy, jail terms for drunk drivers, bans on smoking and cigarette advertisement, and higher taxes on cigarettes. According to Gallup polls taken between 2000 and 2006, women have been and are more likely than men to oppose legalized gambling, drug use, and prostitution (Shiraev and Sobel 2006). In addition, women also have tended to hold on to the more idealized image of political authorities longer than men. During the last 30 years, women have been more likely than men to support Democratic candidates for president: Jimmy Carter in 1976, Bill Clinton in 1992 and 1996, Al Gore in 2000, and John Kerry in 2004 (Shiraev and Sobel 2006).

Studies show that women tend to be more oriented than men toward local political issues, especially those pertaining to schools and education. Men, in contrast, show greater interest in national and international affairs. Women's interests primarily include policies regarding equality, environmental protection, disarmament, education, culture, and social and welfare issues (Norrander 1999; Shiraev and Sobel 2006). Men's interests, however, included economic and industrial policies, energy issues, transportation, national security, and foreign affairs. Young females are significantly more pro-equality than males, especially with regard to ethnic and racial prejudice (Palmer and Simon 2006).

Gender Stereotypes

A remarkable survey (Williams and Best 1990) was conducted in 27 countries in which people were asked to indicate whether particular words (adjectives) were closely associated with men, women, or not associated by gender. A general sex stereotype was present in all cultures. Cross-culturally, including in the United States, such characteristics as dominance, autonomy, aggression, exhibition, and achievement were associated with men. Such traits as nurturance (providing loving care and attention), help in time of distress, reverence, and submissiveness were associated with women. Males were considered more robust, assertive, aggressive, autocratic, forceful, stern, and wise. In the majority of rural developing countries, women were seen as dreamy, sensitive, affectionate, sentimental, and submissive (Williams and Best 1990). In these rural societies, unlike in industrial nations like the United States, the perceived differences between men and women were greater.

Sexism

What is sexism? This is behavior—an action or expressed opinion—that discriminates against women or men based only on their sex or gender characteristics. It is important to make distinctions between sexist behavior and sexist opinions. Sexist behavior is, in fact, discrimination against women or men. Sexist statements, on the other hand, are not necessarily discriminatory, but they are often expressions of deeply embedded stereotypes. However, sexism almost always causes or creates disagreement, no matter how it is displayed, whether it is in someone's actions or words. Here are several examples of sexist actions.

- A professor at a state university announces he will teach a new class in the fall semester. During registration he suggests to several female students who want to sign up for his class that they should take other classes because this class will be too hard for women.

- The chairperson of a student organization on campus—a club that includes both male and female students—says she has to have a deputy. Several male students express their desire to work for this organization; however, the chairperson says that the deputy has to be a female student, because in her opinion, men are not as responsible as women.

- A personnel officer of a security firm wants to hire someone for a building security guard position. One man and one woman apply for the position. Both are equally qualified and have the same level of experience. The manager decides to pick the man because, in his opinion, men make better security guards.

- A manager of a small company needs to hire an assistant. Three people apply for this position: two men and one woman. They all have some experience and are qualified to work in the position. The manager decides to hire the woman because he believes women are better assistants.

- A single mother is denied a promotion in the company for which she works. As she explains it, the manager was afraid that she would miss too many days of work due to her child's potential for illness.

- A newlywed woman's job application is refused on the basis of her marital status. She was told that she could become pregnant very soon, and her absence from work due to pregnancy and the birth of a child would be highly unacceptable to the management.

- A teacher gives different homework assignments to the students in class. Male students receive difficult assignments, and female students receive easier ones. The teacher says that he is doing this because women aren't usually good at this subject.

Sexism stands for the denial of equal opportunity for men and women. However, do not think that any action made in favor of one gender over the other is sexist. For example, behavior in these cases may not be called sexist. A careful observer with a critical mind can detect and understand contextual elements of human behavior.

- A sports club is looking for a person to work as a janitor in the female locker rooms. There is no way for a man to get this position. Why is this not a case of discrimination against men? Because privacy rules require that there should be a woman working in the locker rooms designated for women only.

- No professional football team has ever signed any female players. This is not discrimination against women. Why? Because women can play professionally and because there is a Women's Professional Football League.

- A movie director is looking for actors—men and women—for his new movie. A woman cannot be hired to play a man's role, and a man cannot be hired for a woman's role. (In some films, however, such substitution has been appropriate.)

Sometimes, it can be very difficult to establish whether a sexist act has been committed. People give differing interpretations of situations, and their views are based on their backgrounds, beliefs, and many contextual details. Some examples of such controversial situations are given. What would be your opinion if you are asked to comment on these cases?

- A men's college soccer team needs a goalkeeper for the forthcoming season. Rama, a 19-year-old sophomore, says that she could play for the college team. She feels she has enough soccer experience playing goalie for her high school. Unfortunately, because of financial considerations, the college does not have a female soccer program or team. The coach refuses to accept Rama so the team continues to look for a male goaltender to fill the position.

Is this a case of sexism? On one hand, many of us would suggest that it is absolutely logical to expect that only men should play for men's sports teams. Yet, Rama argues that the college's sports programs are supported by taxpayers' money, and it is fundamentally unfair to deny her membership in the team just because she is a woman. Therefore, her logic may be compelling for many individuals. For example, in Little League baseball, which is designed by local communities specifically for younger children, there are only teams for boys. However, recently it was established in court that girls should not be denied the opportunity (Title IX) to join these baseball teams. Today if you look carefully on the fields where seven- to ten-year-old children are playing baseball, you are likely to see girls playing on the team.

- Anyone who buys a car in the United States must purchase automobile insurance. If a man and a woman own identical cars and their driving records are similar, the man will pay higher monthly premiums than the woman.

Is this discrimination against one sex? Some may readily say yes because the men are required to pay more because of their sex, right? Not completely. According to statistics, men are involved in more destructive automobile accidents than women, and this is costly for the insurance companies. Therefore, men are charged more money by the insurance companies not because they are men, but because they are more dangerous drivers than women.

✎ A Class Exercise

Express your opinion about whether these cases portray sex discrimination. Your opinions are based on your personal experience, beliefs, and values, so there are no correct or incorrect answers.

Case 1. A restaurant owner is looking for a waitress to work evening shifts. This restaurant attracts many single men; therefore, according to the owner's opinion, a waitress (not a waiter) would be good in terms of both sales and tips. The owner has hired men to wait tables before, but he did not like the results.

Case 2. The publisher of a women's magazine is looking for candidates to fill the position of senior editor. Among several qualified applicants there is one man, whose candidacy was rejected outright because the publisher said that a man cannot be an inspirational leader for a women's magazine. The magazine publishes materials related to sensitive women's issues in the United States and the world.

Case 3. Due to a number of circumstances, the department of biology in one private college is composed of six women and no men. All six female professors agree that it would be excellent if the department could hire a man for a new job opening. The selection committee decided to interview only male applicants.

Case 4. A television station in one of the big cities on the East Coast has a tradition of broadcasting the evening news with two news anchors working together in the studio—one man and one woman. When the female anchor is promoted, the station starts looking for a woman with professional experience to fill the position. Any man who applies for the opening will have much less chance of getting the job because the station is looking specifically for a woman.

Sexist Remarks

Perhaps you have heard, *That is a sexist statement,* or *This person has made a sexist remark.* In the opening vignette for this chapter, Sony's views were labeled sexist. What is a sexist remark? How do you recognize sexist remarks and avoid using them?

A sexist statement is an expressed opinion that discriminates between men and women only on the basis of their sex or gender. Quite often the sexist opinion is not based on facts, or the facts are limited or not verifiable. Sexist statements often are very general, simplistic, and may seriously distort the truth about men and women. It is also important to keep in mind that sexist statements typically degrade one sex in favor of the other. Therefore, most sexist statements can be offensive and may cause a change in the way the listeners view the person making the sexist remark. The following are several examples of sexist statements and an explanation of their meaning.

- *Women cannot work under pressure, while men can.* This is a sexist statement because we all know that both sexes can work well under pressure. Moreover, some research suggests that very often women are able to cope with stress better than men do.
- *Women are better parents than men.* This is a sexist statement because there are good fathers and good mothers. Who determines which one is better?
- *Men are irresponsible.* This is an unsupported generalization. What is responsibility, and what is the context of this comment? Is there evidence that most men are irresponsible? The statement is too vague, so is a generalization based on experience or beliefs. It could be considered sexist.

Now consider this sentence: *Women live longer than men.* Although this statement is bad news for most men, it is true. The life expectancy for a woman, around the world, is higher than a man's life expectancy, and the difference can be as much as ten years in some countries! Some facts are difficult to accept.

Affirmative Action

American law prohibits any discrimination of individuals because of their race, color, religion, gender, or national origin. Born during the civil rights movement in the 1960s, affirmative action calls for women and minorities to be given special consideration in employment, education, and business decisions. Judging by the results today, the playing field appears to continue to be tilted very much in favor of white men. Overall, minorities and women are in vastly lower-paying jobs and still face active discrimination in some sectors. The proponents (supporters) of affirmative action say that equal opportunity cannot be just an empty slogan or an expression of good intentions. Equal opportunity should be achieved by legal and political means (Hill 1997). This policy was implemented to increase diversity in business, education, and social activities. Supporters of affirmative action often suggest that many women on the job have to deal with a so-called *glass ceiling,* or the situation where the professional development within an organization is limited simply because of gender discrimination (where a manager does not promote a woman simply because she is a women). In its modern form, affirmative action can call for an admissions officer, faced with two similarly qualified applicants, to choose the minority student over the white student, or for a manager to recruit and hire a qualified woman for a job instead of a man. Defenders of affirmative action say that granting modest advantages to minorities and women is more than fair, given hundreds of years of discrimination that mostly benefited white men.

However, these days an increasingly assertive opposition movement argues that favoring members of one group (women, for example) over another (men, for instance) simply moves discrimination from one group and imposes it on the other. This situation is often called **reverse discrimination.** Critics blame affirmative action for robbing them of promotions and other opportunities. They argue that free competition and the marketplace itself would promote those individuals who can contribute to community and society, without giving these people special treatment.

The U.S. Supreme Court has limited affirmative action and suggested that affirmative action can be used only where there is ongoing discrimination against minorities and women. Some states, California, for example, are moving to abolish affirmative action in education and job recruitment. Behind the rhetoric lies a political and legal quagmire—the changing view in U.S. courts and public opinion of affirmative action, in general, and set-aside programs in particular, which would guarantee certain benefits to specific groups based on quotas. Since 1989 the U.S. Supreme Court has said that city governments may use set-asides only as a last resort and otherwise, the court has said such preferences may not be based on race or gender. In a 2005 decision, the U.S. Supreme Court ruled that universities may use race as a factor in determining students' admission to achieve a diverse student body.

Sexual Harassment

One of the reasons that affirmative action is still considered necessary by some people is because of sexual harassment in the workplace, mostly affecting women. According to The U.S. Equal Employment Opportunity Commission, **sexual harassment** is a form of sex discrimination that violates Title VII of the Civil Rights Act. It typically includes unwelcome sexual advances, requests for sexual favors, and other verbal or physical conduct of a sexual nature. This conduct affects another individual's employment; interferes with his or her work performance; or creates an intimidating, hostile, or offensive work environment. For example, if an employer suggests to an employee that she would get a pay raise or promotion if she would go out with or date the employer, this is an act of sexual harassment.

We have mentioned that freedom of speech is one of the most fundamental freedoms that Americans have. However, there are situations in which particular words are not considered proper and may be rejected and condemned by many people. This is not the government's attempt to restrict free exchange of ideas. On the contrary, certain limitations aim to protect people—and you would be one of them—from harmful words and actions of others. For example, in your communication with other people in the area of human sexuality and male-female relationship, there are general rules you must follow, a violation of which might be considered sexual harassment. Traditionally, international students ask many questions about this issue.

The college or university that you attend will have an institutional policy related to sexual harassment, and it should be highlighted in the student handbook. This is a serious topic on campuses today, and there is little tolerance for sexual harassment. Sexual harassment can occur in a variety of circumstances. Here are some examples:

- *Student R tells a sexual joke (the content of the joke includes mention of male and female genitalia and sexual intercourse) to a group of students, both male and female; most of them do not know Student R well.*

  This joke could be offensive to some or maybe all students in the group—and it does not matter how many male and female students there are in the group. This situation falls into the category of sexual harassment.

- *As Student S walks across campus, he whistles loudly at a beautiful woman passing by.*

  Even though such behavior may be common in many countries, this qualifies as sexual harassment in the United States.

- *Student P talks to a female student he met two days ago, telling her how beautiful and sexy her body is.*

  If two people are not in a relationship, any mention about a woman's body (that includes breasts, hips, legs, lips, and other parts of the body that may represent female sexuality) is inappropriate. This is particularly inappropriate if such comments are made in a public place. The same rule applies to women's comments about men's body parts. Remember, the victim (a person who is harassed) as well as the harasser may be a woman or a man. Boys may be sexually harassed by girls. The victim does not have to be of the opposite sex. In other words, a male can harass another male.

- *Student A (a woman) and Student Y (a man) met in class a month ago. They are not friends. Student A asks Student Y to help her with the homework assignment. Student Y agrees but jokingly suggests that Student A should return the favor in the way that women "always return favors to men."*

Such innuendo about sex, especially as a form of payment for help—even though it is said in the form of a joke—is offensive to another person and causes significant distress. In this case, Student Y uses his knowledge in the academic subject as a form of interpersonal power.

- *Student T tells a student at a party that T is the sexiest man alive because he belongs to a particular ethnic group.*

Again, even though the statement may be considered a tease, it may be seen by some as a direct solicitation of sex. Moreover, because it was said to a particular student directly, it may be interpreted as an act of sexual harassment.

- *Student W makes a public remark about Student J, and says with laughter that Student J might be gay.*

The sexual orientation of another person is his or her private issue and cannot be discussed openly without this individual's explicit consent. Sexual teasing, ridiculing, and mocking are forms of sexual harassment.

- *Student L talks to another student (they met only last week) and touches her neck and ear when they are in line for dinner.*

This is improper behavior. Even though Student L believes that the relationship is going well, he still has to ask first about what is acceptable and what is not in his behavior.

Remember, sexual harassment is not always intentional. It can be unintentional, spontaneous, and designed to be funny. If you say, *I did not want to offend this individual,* it doesn't mean that you are not responsible for your words. In addition, sexual harassment is always interpreted from the victim's standpoint. You may say that your remarks were not inappropriate, but what is judged is the effect of the words! Sexual harassment is not always a direct discrimination or intimidation. It can be subtle, hidden, and covered by words with double meanings.

You may say, *How can I remember all these rules of behavior?* You do not have to remember. What you have to do is understand the ideals behind the rules and agree with them. Then your memory will help you to recall the details. Meanwhile, some useful tips that will help you learn more about sexual harassment are summarized in the box.

It is helpful for a harassment victim to directly inform the harasser that the conduct is unwelcome and must stop. The victim of sexual harassment should not be afraid to complain about a harasser. If you think you are right, do not be afraid that the person you accuse would deny your words. There could be other people who have similar complaints against this individual.

⭐ A Useful Tip

Do not tell sexual jokes or make remarks about other people's sexual activities and body parts associated with sexuality. Do not assume that the rules of communication between men and women that are acceptable in your home country are equally acceptable in the United States. If there is something you cannot comprehend well, talk to your instructors or to those who have lived in the United States for a long time.

A Homework Assignment

Determine which of the following statements are sexist and represent true facts. If you don't know the answer right away, search for facts on the Internet or ask your instructor for assistance.

1. *Women in the United States are more vulnerable to eating disorders than men.*
2. *There are more single mothers in the United States than single fathers.*
3. *There are more violent criminals among men than among women.*
4. *Women do not drive as well as men.*

CHAPTER 9

Understanding Ethnicity, Race, and Religion in the United States

How different are people living in different countries?

- In Sierra Leone, West Africa, during hunting some men do not call each other by name because they are afraid that the devils might learn the names and harm people.
- In traditional Islamic countries, many people believe in demons, who might possess the human body and cause psychological disorders.

It's possible that people in New York or Los Angeles would think that these kinds of beliefs are naïve. However, national surveys (Gallup and FOX News) reveal that in the United States, 24 percent of those surveyed said they believed in the existence of witches, and 40 percent said they believed that it's possible to be possessed by the devil (Shiraev and Levy 2007).

- In Hong Kong, people throw notes attached to oranges into a "wishing tree," hoping that if a thrown wish "hooks" onto a branch, it will come true. If you are not from Hong Kong, you might consider this an unusual custom, but in the United States, people regularly throw coins (money!) into fountains and into the ocean to make wishes. Many Americans also use talismans to protect themselves from harm (for example, some people wear amulets), abstain from saying bad things about other people (fearing bad luck), avoid numbers (such as 13), and knock on wood for luck.

Americans' behaviors and beliefs are similar and different from those from other countries and cultures. We all see things in a unique way, yet similarly. We are different because we had different experiences growing up and different resources available to us; we ate different foods, learned from different textbooks, and pledged our allegiance to different flags. But we are similar because we are human beings who share an understanding of the many common elements to being a human being. Ethnicity, race, and religion sometimes set boundaries and creates walls between and among people, but every day, we must recognize and understand the similarities that connect us.

Race and Ethnicity

Racial and ethnic identities are very important issues for Americans. Such identities are frequently sources of pride, strength, and dignity. What meaning do people in the United States attach to the words *race, nationality,* and *ethnicity?* First, there is no one meaning or "correct" understanding of these terms. As is true for many words and expressions, usage is based on how people interpret them at a certain point in history. Therefore—and also because American sociologists and anthropologists are still debating the definitions of race and ethnicity—we will introduce the most common views on these issues. It must be understood from the beginning of this study that race and ethnicity are significant, powerful, and emotionally charged issues in the United States, and that much of the current social commentary and controversy surrounds these issues.

Race is typically defined as a group of people distinguished by certain similar and genetically transmitted physical characteristics. It is essential to comment on the high or low frequency of occurrence of such physical characteristics because all physical traits appear in all populations. For example, some Germans have frizzy hair, and some Africans have red hair. There are many dark-skinned European Americans and light-skinned African Americans. Many American experts, however, suggest that race is better described and understood as a social category because *race* indicates particular experiences shared by many people who belong to a category of people (Gould 1997). Some people have proposed to abandon this word altogether, while others offer to use the word *origin* (for example, African, European, etc.) instead of race.

Today in the United States, the government, as well many private organizations and agencies, often asks anybody who applies for a job to identify their race or origin. Several such standard categories are identified:

White or **Caucasian** (includes people of European, Arab, and Central Asian origin)

Black or **African American** (includes people of African origin)

Native American (includes people of American Indian, Eskimo, and Aleut origin)

Asian (includes people of East Asian and Pacific Islander origin)

Hispanic (includes those whose origin is Chicano, Mexican, Mexican-American, Cuban, Spaniard, Puerto Rican, or from the Spanish-speaking countries of South or Central America or the Caribbean)

As you see, the Hispanic category incorporates people of many racial groups. How many people of each race or group of origin live in the United States? Some estimates made by the U.S. Bureau of Census—a government organization that provides statistical analysis of American population—are presented.

TABLE 9.1 U.S. Population in 2000 and 2050

Race/Origin	2000	2050
All races	282,000,000	420,000,000
White, non-Hispanic	196,000,000	210,000,000
Black, African American	36,000,000	61,000,000
Hispanic-Latino	36,000,000	103,000,000
Asian	10,700,000	33,400,000
Other (including Native Americans, Pacific Islanders, and mixed races)	7,075,000	22,437,000

Source: U.S. Bureau of the Census, 2007.

Does the place of our birth make us different in terms of behavior, emotions, or values? Specialists in human behavior say no. What makes us relatively different—or relatively similar—is our experiences accumulated during childhood, adolescence, and adulthood. We are all born with the basic dispositions created by an interplay of genetic factors. We then develop our individual attitudes, skills, and other attributes under the influence of the culture and environment. Biological factors—for example, the way our nervous systems function—constitute the *foundation* for our behavior. Social and cultural factors, childhood experiences, the overall situation in society, family practices, education, traditions, and many other influences may determine who we are as adults.

For example, Ramesh was born to his dark-skinned and dark-haired parents from India. His hair and skin are dark, too. Ramesh's parents speak English with an Indian accent. He speaks the language without a detectable accent and pronounces English almost like a national news broadcaster. Although Ramesh's parents adhere to many traditional Indian values and beliefs, Ramesh in most ways reflects typical beliefs and customs of American teenagers.

One of the most significant factors that affects human lives everywhere and creates disparities of many kinds among people is the availability of resources and money. Higher income, for example, guarantees better opportunity. If Mary has better opportunities in life than Susan does—a better house, higher-quality food, greater access to educational opportunities—then Mary has a higher potential for a higher-paying job. More opportunity can produce higher income. Higher income creates more opportunities for those who earn this income compared to those who do not. Table 9.2 compares median household incomes of American families.

TABLE 9.2. Estimates of Median* Income per Household, 2007

All Races	$39,509
White or Caucasian	$40,422
Black or African American	$32,021
Asian and Pacific Islander	$42,109
Hispanic	$27,266

Source: U.S. Census Bureau, Current Population Survey. Median scores in this table indicate that 50 percent of the families in each category make more than the median score, and 50 percent of the families make less than the median score.
*Median is the value that describes the middle value of a group of statistics.

Which group in the United States has the highest income per family? Which group has the lowest? In general, who would have better economic opportunities in the United States?

Because various social groups share common experience—such as wealth or poverty, norms, symbols, religion, values, and memories—the individuals of a particular group are expected to have some typical psychological traits that are somewhat different from the members of another culture or group. However, human groups are extremely diverse, and there are tremendous behavioral variations within them. For instance, although American culture is considered as a whole to be materialistic and individualistic, there are many philanthropic and idealistic individuals. Likewise, in primarily collectivist cultures, one can find selfish, greedy, and arrogant individuals.

In the United States, the term *ethnicity* usually describes your cultural heritage, the experience shared by people who have a common ancestral origin, language, and traditions, and often, religion and geographic territory. A *nation* is defined as a people who share common geographical origin, history, and language, and are unified as a political entity—an independent state recognized by other countries. For example, those who acquire the status of a national of the United States—become citizens—are either born in the United States or become citizens through a naturalization process.

The words *race, ethnicity,* and *nationality* are used differently in other countries. What is often labeled as *race* or *ethnicity* in the United States is termed *nationality* in other countries. For example, if Ron, who refers to himself as being an African American, marries Lilia, who refers to herself as a Latina (a popular description of one's Hispanic origin), their marriage would be labeled an interracial marriage in the United States. The same marriage would be labeled either cross-national or international in some other countries. Moreover, one can easily find racial categories common in the United States that are not recognized in other countries.

Human groups are constantly moving and mixing with others. In the United States, perhaps more frequently than in other countries, people have freedom to choose what cultural identity they want or have and what group they want themselves to be identified with. Phenomena such as ethnic or national identity are becoming increasingly dynamic and are based on different interests, ideas, and individual choices.

✎ A Class Exercise

Ethnicity and Nationality in the United States

It is important to realize that the United States, like most nations, is made up of many different ethnic groups. Similarly, there can be different national groups within an ethnic group. To help lessen your confusion, read on.

Same nationality, different ethnic groups.

Martha and Martin are both U.S. citizens. Nationally, they are both Americans. However, ethnically, Martha is Brazilian because her parents emigrated to the United States from Brazil when she was a little girl, and she received her citizenship a few years ago. Martin is a seventh-generation New Yorker. His ethnic roots are mixed: Irish, French, German, and Russian.

Same ethnic groups, different nationality.

Hamed and Aziza are both Palestinian exchange students living in New Jersey. Hamed's parents live in Tel-Aviv, and he and his parents are Israeli citizens. Aziza does not have a permanent nationality even though she holds a Jordanian passport.

These complex examples are common in the United States, and many people feel more regional identity than national or ethnic attachments. Be careful what assumptions you make about a person based on these factors.

Language influences our attitudes about other people and affects our evaluation of different ethnic groups. Americans, as you know, enjoy one of the most fundamental civil liberties—the freedom of speech. In particular, it is against the law for the government—with some exceptions, like threats to other people's lives—to punish Americans citizens, residents, and guests for what they say, write, or wear. However, there are many cultural norms and standards that suggest the type of words considered appropriate, and what words are perceived as offensive and, therefore, inappropriate. Most colleges and universities have regulations that limit the use of offensive language in the classroom—called ethnic or racial slurs—particularly if the person is using the words in attempt to offend other individuals. One must be *very* careful when referring to racial groups in a public dialogue, as it is easy to offend someone by using an outdated or inappropriate term.

☆ A Useful Tip

Learn how people label ethnic groups and groups of origin (race). Enjoy the freedom of speech; however, be sensitive to what other people feel about certain words and expressions about them. You may hurt others without intending to. Ask questions, like "Is it okay to use this word?" Some people do not like to be labeled by ethnic categories, but prefer to be referred to by the country of their origin, for example, Brazilian, Korean, or Nigerian, but not Latino, Asian, or African.

Religious Beliefs

Religion gives many of us meaning and purpose in life. It teaches us about the most appropriate rules of conduct and provides us with powerful self-restraint against inappropriate behavior. Religious beliefs help us cope with many tragic situations in life and give us an emotional boost during personal defeat, failure, or downfall. Religious beliefs are inspirational, and they help overcome obstacles and keep our hopes alive.

Almost 90 percent of Americans identify with a specific religion (Institute for Social Research 1972–2004). The United States is home to many of the world's religions. The Pilgrims, the first European settlers in America, came to this country with a particular religious vision. In Europe, many of them had been subjected to discrimination, persecution, and—quite often—death. Today, as throughout American history, individuals who are persecuted in their home countries for their religious beliefs and practices can receive asylum (safety) in the United States.

Which religions have the most followers in this country today?

TABLE 9.3. Some Major U.S. Religious Bodies

Religious Body	Number of Members
Protestant (Christian)	85–87 million
Roman Catholic Church (Christian)	62–65 million
Muslim	1.6–4 million
Orthodox Christian (Russian, Greek, Ethiopian, and others)	5–6 million
Jewish	5–6 million
Church of Jesus Christ of Latter-Day Saints (Mormon)	4–4.5 million
Buddhist	1.8–2 million
Hindu	Approx. 1 million

Source: Numbers and assessments are based on the following: Yearbook of American & Canadian Churches (2007); U.S. Bureau of the Census, (2006); National Jewish Population Survey (2002); Religious Congregations and Membership (2000). When the direct count is unavailable, assessments are made by different groups based on different criteria.

Citizens in the United States have the right to choose any religion or no religion. The U.S. Constitution permits private religious activity in colleges and universities. However, certain rules and regulations apply to any religious activity in the United States, and these rules are generally the same for both public and private schools. However, some private institutions of higher education may have their own guidelines about religious behavior on their campuses (Cherry, DeBerg, and Porterfield 2001).

All in all, government and religion are separated in the United States. Therefore, state-funded colleges and universities will not have courses in their curricula designed to promote any particular religion. However, you may find courses on the history of religion, comparative religion, and others that teach about the role of religion in the history of the United States and other countries.

You have the right to pray individually or in groups. You are free to discuss any religious views with your peers, as long as these discussions do not disrupt public order. You can enjoy the right to read any religious scripture, say "grace" before meals, pray before tests, and discuss religion. However, your school activities come first. For example, you should not pray during the test for an hour and then ask your professor for extra time to finish the test.

You express your religious beliefs in the form of projects and reports, and no one should reject your work because of its religious content, such as quotes, symbols, and examples. However, your work should be relevant to the assignment given to you. Follow the instructions and guidelines. These guidelines usually mention the grading criteria for your work, such as substance, relevance, appearance, and grammar. For example, if your sociology professor gives an assignment to find and compare suicide rates in several countries, you may not claim an exemption from the assignment because suicide is strongly prohibited by your religion.

If, during a class discussion, you are asked about a particular military action, and if you oppose that action based solely on your religious beliefs, can you make religious remarks on the issue? Yes, you can. Your remarks during classroom discussion constitute your expression of free speech. Similarly, you can criticize religion and promote atheism. Your professor may not silence you just because you make critical statements against religion. However, do not forget that other students also have the right to speak, and they may criticize your views, too.

> **☆ A Useful Tip**
>
> Any criticism against a particular religion should not become excessive. In this case, such criticism may be called religious harassment.

You also have the right to distribute religious literature to your schoolmates, but you are supposed to do this only in a particular place at particular times. Use common sense and talk to professors and counselors outside of the classroom if you have problems or unanswered questions about religion on campus.

You are protected by law to observe and speak to others about the religious holidays you celebrate. You can talk about religious traditions, practices, and the history of particular religious holidays. Feel free to invite other students to join you in your celebration. However, if students decline your invitation, do not insist because it may be considered harassment. As you see, harassment can be of two types: pro- and anti-religion.

Religious messages on t-shirts, shirts, and hats are not generally prohibited on campus. Students may wear religious attire, such as crosses, yarmulkes, turbans, and head scarves. If your religious beliefs do not allow you to wear gym clothes because they are too revealing, you cannot be forced to do so.

In many cases, your school will excuse you for participation in religious celebrations and rituals, especially if they require your absence from school. However, the school is not obligated to do so, and if you miss a test or an assignment, you will be held accountable. Do not assume that your particular religious practices will be given priority over the published academic schedule. A brief list of common religious holidays is outlined in Table 9.4.

TABLE 9.4 Common Religious Holidays*

Religious Holiday	Brief Description
Chanukah (Jewish) December 3–11	In 179 BCE, the Maccabees led a group of Jews in battle against invading warriors who had desecrated the Temple and extinguished its eternal light. After winning the battle, legend has it that they found a single cruse of oil, which miraculously lasted eight days, until more could be found. The Chanukah menorah is lit for eight nights to celebrate the miracle. Chanukah was declared a holiday by Judah Maccabee and his followers to celebrate the rededication of the Temple. Gifts are exchanged, and foods fried in oil are customary.
Christmas (Christian) December 25	This is the celebration of the birth of Jesus Christ, the Son of God, according to Christian beliefs. Many Christians attend a midnight Mass or other Christmas Eve services at churches that are usually decorated with poinsettias, candles, and greenery. Families try to gather for Christmas, making this a busy time to travel.
Easter (Christian) The exact day of Easter varies each year but always falls between March 22 and April 25.	Easter celebrates the resurrection of Jesus Christ, a joyous occasion in Christianity. According to Christian beliefs, after Jesus was crucified by the Romans and buried, his tomb was found empty. An angel told his followers that Jesus had risen and ascended into heaven. Many churches hold sunrise services on Easter Sunday to symbolize the return of light to the world after Jesus' resurrection. The day is observed with feasts and celebrations. Easter also marks the end of Lent. One of the popular Easter customs is decorating and coloring hard-boiled eggs.
Ramadan (Muslim) Occurs in the ninth month of the Islamic lunar calendar, around November	Ramadan is the most sacred holiday of the Muslim year and the holy month of fasting. Fasting is considered to be a very important form of religious obligation of Islam and provides many benefits, including learning self-control. During this period, Muslims must abstain from food, drink, and sexual intercourse from dawn until dusk each day. Ramadan is a time of worship, reading the Qur'an, charitable acts, atonement, and the purification of individual behavior. Ramadan ends with the Festival of Fast-Breaking, which is a joyous celebration marked by a special gift of charity. Muslims dress in holiday apparel and attend a community prayer in the morning.
Yom Kippur (Jewish) Celebration usually in mid-September	Yom Kippur is the holiest day in the Jewish calendar. The observance is also known as the Day of Atonement since the events of Yom Kippur focus on asking and granting forgiveness for one's wrongdoings. Yom Kippur falls at the end of the ten Days of Penitence, a period that begins with Rosh Hashanah, the Day of Judgment. Jews attend services at a synagogue or temple on the eve and day of Yom Kippur. On Yom Kippur, Jews perform no work and abstain from food, drink, and sex.
Mawlid (Muslim) 12th day of the month of Rabi al-Awwal in the Muslim lunar calendar	Mawlid al-Nabi is a celebration of the birthday of the Prophet Muhammad, founder of Islam. Muhammad was born about CE 570 and died in BCE 632. The Mawlid al-Nabi was first observed around the 13th century and was preceded by a month of celebration. The actual day of Muhammad's birthday includes a sermon, recitation of litanies, honoring of religious dignitaries, gift-giving, and a feast.
Diwali (Hindu) 15th day of Kartika	Diwali is a five-day festival. The celebration means as much to Hindus as Christmas does to Christians. Diwali means "rows of lighted lamps," and the celebration is often referred to as the Festival of Lights. During this time, homes are thoroughly cleaned, lamps are lit, and windows are opened to welcome Laksmi, goddess of wealth. Candles and lamps are lit as a greeting to Laksmi. Gifts are exchanged, and festive meals are prepared. Because there are many regions in India, there are also many manifestations of the Diwali festival.

*Sunset times are calculated for Kansas City. Kansas uses the Sunrise/Sunset/Twilight and Moonrise/Moonset/Phase website provided by the Time Service Dept., U.S. Naval Observatory, which is the official source of time used in the United States.

For more information about federal and state rules and regulations regarding religious activities on campus, contact your school's counseling center or department of education at your state.

Stereotypes and the Power of Generalizations

We often do not have enough time or patience to analyze every event we encounter, or every person we are dealing with. We categorize or "pigeon hole" and classify almost everybody we see or communicate with. Such clear-cut opinions about other people are called stereotypes based on generalizations. In particular, a stereotype is a categorical assumption that all members of a given group have similar distinctive traits. Some people say, "all Mexicans like rhythm," or "all Canadians play hockey," or "all Americans care only about money." Of course, not all Mexicans love rhythm, many Canadians do not like hockey, and not every American considers money his or her only concern in life! But stereotypes can become dangerous when they become more critical or demeaning. Such statements as "most illegal immigrants are criminals," or "interracial marriages are less stable than same-race marriages," or "all Jews are wealthy" may be expressed in our daily judgments despite the fact that they are basically wrong.

You may think that because stereotypes are really descriptions of large groups of people, one should not be offended by them. But when we apply stereotypes to individuals on the basis of national, ethnic, religious, or some other group affiliation, we can offend people. Think about how you would feel if someone judged you based on your skin color or ethnicity and only that.

A Case in Point

People often do not realize the extent to which they distort information when they stereotype. When Britain's Prince Phillip was visiting a high-tech company near Edinburgh, Scotland, in 1999, he spotted a poorly wired fuse box and consequently made a remark to the company manager: "It looks as though it was put in by an Indian." The royal spokesperson apologized for the remark, but you can imagine how offensive it was to millions of hard-working and high-achieving Indians and their descendants living around the world.

In 2005, Mexican President Vicente Fox commented that Mexican immigrants to the United States take jobs "that not even blacks want to do." The Mexican president's office immediately issued a statement saying the president had misspoken and people should not interpret his words in a wrong way. Of course, the president did not want to offend blacks; he should have chosen his words more carefully.

Why Do Stereotypes Occur?

Stereotypes arise largely out of our lack of knowledge. Many stereotypes are produced because we often move no further in our communications than the first impression. People's looks are the easiest to recognize at a first glance. Therefore, some national, ethnic, or racial characteristics appear to be more clear and notable than other characteristics, such as education, age, or social class (Gudykunst and Bond 1997). If a person feels angry or frustrated, negative stereotypes about other people come to mind easily. Moreover, we often use stereotypes to justify particular negative feelings about other individuals (Zaller 1992).

Think
Critically

The following is a description of interpersonal communications of "typical" American, Japanese, and Arab individuals adopted from a best-selling book (Fast 1988).

There are distinct differences in the way an American, Japanese, and an Arab individual handle his or her personal "territory." In Japan, crowding together is a sign of warm and pleasant intimacy. Like the Japanese, the Arabs tend to cling close to one another. Arabs' houses are generally large and empty, with the people clustering together in one small area. Arabs do not like to be alone, so that partitions between rooms are usually avoided. The Arab likes to touch his companion, feel him. The Japanese avoid touching, however, and prefer to keep physical boundaries. Typical Americans set "boundaries" in public. They avoid pushing or intruding into the space of another person. Americans very seldom shove, push, and pinch other people in public. Arabs have no concept of privacy in a public place. When two Arabs talk to each other, they look each other in the eyes with great intensity. The same intensity is rarely exhibited in the American culture.

Question. Do you think all these statements are stereotypical? Or maybe you suggest that these judgments are somewhat accurate. How should we draw a line between being accurate and being stereotypical?

Is it possible to reduce the impact of stereotypical judgments about other people? We hope so. To do so successfully, let us better understand stereotypical judgment itself.

We make at least two mistakes when we make stereotypical judgments. In the course of evaluating similarities and differences between two groups, we often:

✓ allow genuine differences to be obscured by similarities

✓ allow genuine similarities to be obscured by differences

Stereotyping is, in fact, permitting similarities between phenomena to eclipse their differences. Those who stereotype other individuals and groups are prone to automatically overestimate "in-group" similarities, while minimizing (or even ignoring) "in-group" differences. In other words, the individual perceives group members to be more alike than they really are (for example, people of this ethnic group are always late for class) and, at the same time, does not recognize many of the ways in which they are different from one another (there are plenty of students in this ethnic group who are never late).

Moreover, groups we like and groups we do not like are seen as more different than they really are. In its most extreme form of stereotyping, all members of the particular "out-group" are seen as essentially the same, while their individuality goes virtually unnoticed.

Consider, for example, interpersonal interaction. Imagine you meet a person from an ethnic group that is different from yours. You may perceive a man or woman from this group as basically the same as every other individual from that group. In this way, you view people as not being distinct and varied individuals with separate and unique life experiences, memories, feelings, perceptions, values, beliefs, hopes, fears, and dreams. Instead, these traits are spontaneously filtered through your own sociocultural stereotypes, from which they emerge as Koreans, African Americans, Jews, Latino, Vietnamese, and so on.

Stereotyping is making erroneous, mistaken judgments. However, do not reject the possibility that people can share similar behavior, emotions, or attitudes. How many times have you heard someone make the following pronouncement (or any derivation thereof): "You cannot compare these two people (from two different ethnic groups, for instance) because they are totally and completely different from each other!" This is a vivid illustration of someone making the converse mistake of allowing similarities between people to be overshadowed by their differences. In fact, we can compare groups in search of similarities between people.

Similarly, counselors who say "every student should be viewed and treated as totally unique and without regard to his or her cultural background," runs the risk of allowing true—and potentially helpful—similarities between persons to be overlooked.

Think
Critically

Looking for both similarities and differences can be constructively applied in the cross-cultural counseling setting. For instance, members of the same cultural group may be different in virtually every personality trait. And despite apparent drastic differences, two individuals may share things in common. Consider the following brief vignette as an example of a search for commonalities in two people.

Student: "There's no way that you can understand how I feel. After all, you are American, and I'm not. And you've never been discriminated against because of your nationality."

Counselor: "You are right. I can never know exactly what that feels like. We are truly different in that respect. But at the same time, I know what it's like to be discriminated against because of my religion. And I have had the experience of being persecuted out of ignorance and hatred. To that extent, we do share a common experience. We are indeed both similar and different."

⭐ A Useful Tip

What we might anticipate from an individual based on our expectations does not often match with who he or she really is. Be prepared for such inconsistency between expectations and reality!

⭐ A Useful Tip

When faced with a discrepancy between your opinion and the facts, resist the natural tendency to assume that you are right and the facts must somehow be wrong. That is, ask yourself directly in what ways your opinion might be wrong.

Is it possible to eliminate stereotypes? It is possible to reduce the influence of stereotypes on our daily judgments if one accepts the view that human diversity could be greater than human sameness. Do not underestimate the extent to which your prior beliefs and knowledge can affect your current experience. Generalizations, especially concerning personality characteristics of members of other ethnic or religious groups, cannot be objective, impartial, or neutral. Become aware of your own personal values and biases about particular countries, religions, and ethnic groups. Avoid presenting your value judgments as objective reflections of truth. Remember that most ethnicity-related phenomena—such as traits, attitudes, and beliefs—stretch out along a continuum; thus, it is both artificial and inaccurate to group them into categories! Stereotypes are often based on lack of knowledge and human ignorance. Open your mind, read, watch, listen, learn, educate yourself, travel, communicate—and you will reduce the impact of stereotypes on your life.

CHAPTER 10

Understanding the American Media: Newspapers, Radio, Television, and the Internet

W*hat you watch, listen to, and read tells a lot about the type of person you are. The average adult American spends almost 1,500 hours a year watching television. Radio was estimated to consume 1,100 hours, recorded music 235 hours, and newspapers 175 hours. National Opinion Research Center at the University of Chicago found that 26 percent of Americans in 2006 spent an average of two hours a day and another 15 percent spent three hours a day in front of television. More than 50 percent of Americans in the mid-2000s spent at least one hour a day on the Internet according to the Gallup Poll®. (All data from Shiraev and Sobel 2006.)*

This chapter examines the media like television, radio, the Internet, and newspapers, communication that is technologically capable of reaching most people in the country and is readily affordable to most.

Some people admire a wide variety of choices offered by the media, but others think it is too intrusive and dangerous. No matter which view you take, the media can help you understand Americans and the United States. To learn and to improve your language skills, rather than just sitting and consuming the information, be an active observer, reader, and listener.

Special courses offered in many universities teach students about the American media. You will learn more about the subject, its history, development, and current status when you take such a course, but here we will examine press, radio, and television only as educational sources and suggest how to use them wisely for your personal development.

Mass Media and Business

Most facets of the American media are privately owned. Of course, public (not private) television and radio do exist in America; they are supported by local non-profit organizations or are governmentally funded, like PBS television and National Public Radio (NPR). Public media is not powerful enough to compete with private broadcasting corporations that can make billions of dollars a year. How do private media companies make so much money? Revenues that keep newspaper, TV, and radio business alive come almost exclusively from advertising. Commercial time and space are sold in America like any other product. Private newspapers, television and radio networks, and local stations need to have audiences: the more viewers, listeners, and readers, the better and more profit. Companies want to advertise their products to as many potential buyers as possible. If many people, for example, watch a program, the advertisers will pay more money to run their commercials on this show. Therefore, it is more expensive to advertise during some programs or in some newspapers than in others. A local newspaper will charge only a few dollars for an advertisement, whereas big-market papers such as the *New York Times*, the *Washington Post*, or *USA Today* will charge thousands of dollars.

Popularity Ratings

Newspapers can easily measure their popularity by counting how many copies are sold during a month or a year. The popularity of radio or television can also be measured. For example, two companies in the United States use scientific methods to estimate the number of people tuned in to various television channels and programs. One company, Arbitron, has an agreement with 2,400 families across the country to record what they watch and when in special logbooks. The other company, A.C. Nielsen, installs special electronic devices in the television sets of 1,700 volunteers. These devices record when the television is turned on and what channel is viewed. In other words, these randomly selected people, representing all ages, professions, incomes, and ethnic and racial groups in the United States, give information that reflects viewers' interests in various television programs. Broadcasting companies learn from these reports not only what is most popular, but also which groups—men, women, and children—like what type of programming and what works for evening and for morning audiences. Then advertising takes this into consideration. Beer is advertised primarily in the evening and during sports events to capture the audience most likely to buy that product. Toys and games are usually advertised during afternoons and early evenings, and primarily during children's shows. Evenings are more popular among the viewers than afternoons. Weekends attract larger audiences than weekdays (Graber 2006).

What are some of the most popular television programs in the United States? In the 2000s among the most popular television programs in the United States were *American Idol, CSI: Crime Scene Investigation, NFL Monday Night Football, Friends, Survivor, Desperate Housewives,* and *Who Wants to Be a Millionaire?* Every year, one event always has the most viewers: the Super Bowl, the final professional football championship game of the season, which takes place in early February.

Government Regulations

Some people believe that the American media outlets are overly preoccupied with sensationalism, sex, and violence. Others say that this is okay because the business is regulated by the laws of supply and demand, which means that if you want to see a particular program, you turn your TV on, and if you dislike the program, you change the channel or turn off the TV. Media companies try to create and select only such programming that will attract larger audiences, so that advertisers will pay more money for commercial time. If nobody wants to see a show, sponsors will not pay for advertisement time on that show, and if there is no money, there will be no television program.

In theory, the government cannot say what should be broadcast on radio and television or what should be published in newspapers. This does not mean that American broadcasters who want to get as large of an audience as possible can say and display whatever they want. Although freedom of speech is guaranteed by the U.S. Constitution, the media are subject to a variety of governmental rules and regulations. Broadcasting on radio and television is regulated by a government agency called the Federal Communications Commission (FCC). All media are subject to *libel* laws that hold broadcasters responsible for presenting false information that defames or harms others. In addition to federal regulations, all media are subject to local laws regarding *obscenity*. Therefore, nudity, extreme violence, and verbal profanity are banned from most public programming. In cases of controversial events, public discussions, or elections, television stations try to provide equal time to all sides participating in the issue. Personal attacks aired on television typically result in the attacked person having an opportunity to respond. One cannot advertise cigarettes and tobacco products or hard alcohol beverages like cognac or vodka. If a station or company violates such rules, it can be penalized financially or be forced out of business. Since 1998, all television networks have been required to attach special ratings to their programming indicating potentially disturbing aspects (such as violence, sex, and language), and informing parents whether or not the program is suitable for children of a particular age. (This is similar to movie ratings: R for adult content, PG for parental guidance, and G for general.)

Newspapers

The first daily newspaper in the United States began publication in Philadelphia in 1783. Newspapers once were expensive and reached only a limited number of people. With the improvement of paper manufacturing and the invention of the steam-driven printing press, newspapers became cheaper and thus more affordable to average citizens. By the 1830s, publications like *The New York Sun,* which cost only one penny, arrived and brought a new era of the media in the United States. Still, most early American newspapers were supported by different political parties and groups. Politicians used particular newspapers that were loyal to them to broadcast their political ideas. Only by the end of the 19th century did the independent press begin to develop. Most daily newspapers paid special attention to local news. Only the more expensive, weekly publications focused on national and international news. With the growth of competition, newspapers began to pay attention to sensationalizing their stories. It was discovered that stories about violence, crime, scandals, and sex could be sold very well (Campbell 2006). The term *yellow journalism,* which first appeared in the 1880s, stands for low-quality sensationalist journalism.

The demands of free-market competition caused continuous changes in the newspaper industry. Today, there are few afternoon newspapers; morning newspapers dominate the market. Business mergers have led to most cities being served by only one or two major newspapers. Some specialists suggest that contemporary American newspapers are homogeneous and less politically influenced in their coverage of the news. Why has this happened? Newspaper owners want to sell their publications to larger audiences and, thus, try not to be partisan on particular political and ideological issues.

In many respects, American newspapers are huge corporations that are managed according to the laws and traditions of big business. Such large city papers as the *New York Times,* the *Washington Post,* and the *Los Angeles Times* have millions of subscribers. Such national newspapers as *USA Today* and the *Wall Street Journal* reportedly have a daily circulation of more than 4 million. Popular weekly news magazine such as *Time, Newsweek,* and *U.S. News &*

World Report each sell more than 10 million copies per week (see Table 10.1). The magazines that discuss politics and public policy are *New Republic, National Review, Foreign Affairs, Atlantic Monthly,* and the *New Yorker.*

TABLE 10.1. Average Paid Weekday Circulation of the Top 20 U.S. Newspapers, 2007

1. *USA Today*	2,278,022
2. *The Wall Street Journal*	2,062,312
3. *The New York Times*	1,120,420
4. *The Los Angeles Times*	815,723
5. *New York Post*	724,748
6. *New York Daily News*	718,174
7. *The Washington Post*	699,130
8. *The Chicago Tribune*	566,827
9. *The Houston Chronicle*	503,114
10. *The Arizona Republic*	433,731
11. *The Dallas Morning News*	411,919
12. *Newsday, Long Island*	398,231
13. *The San Francisco Chronicle*	386,564
14. *The Boston Globe*	382,503
15. *The Star-Ledger of Newark, NJ*	372,629
16. *The Atlanta Journal-Constitution*	357,399
17. *The Philadelphia Inquirer*	352,593
18. *The Star Tribune of Minneapolis-St. Paul*	345,252
19. *The Plain Dealer* (Cleveland)	344,704
20. *The Detroit Free Press*	329,989

Source: The Associated Press, 2007.

✐ A Class Assignment

Examine different styles used by newspapers by comparing, for example, the *New York Times* and the *Wall Street Journal*. Take a copy of each published on the same day. First, compare their front pages. Do you find any difference in terms of headline topics? Compare how many photographs each of the two newspapers displays. Do these newspapers cover local news? Compare how international topics are covered. What do these papers say about political issues? Looking at the paper contents, can you figure out who each paper's typical reader is?

   As you will notice, both the *New York Times* and the *Wall Street Journal* are serious daily newspapers that cover national and local politics, international developments, cultural and social events, and entertainment. The style of both newspapers tends to be serious and formal (with exceptions, of course). These newspapers do not dedicate space to gossip and try to provide the information and the analysis of serious issues.

Radio

The first American radio stations were established in the 1920s and quickly became popular. With their appearance, the newspaper monopoly on mass communications began to disappear. Today in the United States, according to the FCC, more than 13,000 radio stations reach about 80 percent of the population. Practically every American household has a radio, and most cars also have one as well. Radio is available inexpensively, compared to television or newspapers. Focusing primarily on local news, weather, traffic reports, and music, radio has changed somewhat from the 1980s because of the rapid increase in the number of talk shows. Sure, this format was popular 50 years ago; however, the rapid development of satellite technology has eliminated geographical barriers, and many talk shows reached the national market. A radio talk show host (sometimes there are two or more such hosts) spends three or four hours in front of the studio microphone. Most of these shows encourage the listeners to call in to ask questions or make comments. This talk show radio format is the sixth most popular format behind pop music, country music, religious music, and "oldies" (music of the 1950s, 1960s, and 1970s) programs. Since the end of the 1980s, political talk shows have also become increasingly popular. NPR, for example, is a non-commercial network that offers non-partisan discussions and analyses of domestic and international news. Today, XM and other satellite-based radio are popular. Their impact on the media and distribution of information remains uncertain.

TV Networks, TV Stations, and Cable Companies

Many students say they are confused about American television. Indeed, it is a very complex conglomerate driven both by public demands and private interests. But despite its complexity, television can be explained in a simple way.

You may have heard the terms *network, cable,* and *television station* many times and wonder if they really have different meanings. Television stations are often called local stations, companies that send signals through airwaves directly to your television antenna. Although a part of private industry, television stations are subject to heavy government regulation. Due to technical problems related to transmission and interference of television signals, the number of stations that a city or town can have is limited. Thus, big cities like New York, Los Angeles, or Chicago can have no more than ten stations. Smaller cities are allowed fewer stations.

It is becoming more and more difficult to receive many TV stations by using an antenna on a TV. Stations are broadcasting now in digital and in high-definition formats. To get quality reception, a cable or satellite service is necessary. *Cable companies,* unlike TV stations, do not send signals directly to individual homes. Cable systems broadcast signals directly to a community antenna. Then the signal is sent by wire to individual homes. According to government regulations, cable companies have to carry local stations. In addition, they can offer a huge variety of channels from other cities. Satellite technology has created opportunities for cable companies to broadcast and receive programs from around the world. Cable television reaches almost 70 percent of American households. Overall, there are about 3,000 broadcast television stations (Graber 2006).

Television networks are private organizations based on contracts composed of a large number of stations called *affiliates.* Television networks offer their affiliates various programs ranging from soap operas and movies to talk shows and football games. Each station decides what kind of local or network programs to air. The biggest American networks—NBC (National Broadcasting Company), CBS (Columbia Broadcasting System), and ABC (American Broadcasting Company)—were founded more than 55 years ago. For many decades, the "big three" dominated American television, competing only with each other. Recently, the competition increased with the emergence of the Fox television network; many cable stations like TBS, TNT, and WGN; and the cable news station CNN.

So what are you watching when you turn on your television? If you do not have cable service, you will be watching what is offered by your local stations: a mix of local news combined with programming offered by networks. In most places today, you will have access to at least four stations. Cable service is relatively expensive and may cost you from $30 to $100 a month. In most university dormitories, students pay for cable themselves. If you decide to pay, your local cable company will plug your television into the company's antenna. In exchange, you will be able to receive from 50 to 400 or more channels, including all local stations.

Television, Radio, and Language Proficiency

Television and radio are great educational sources, so be prepared to learn from them. Many interesting shows and programs are aired when you are not at home; so ideally, you must have a VCR, DVR, or TIVO. If you do not have any of these devices, it is not a problem: It is always fine to ask somebody you know to record a program for you and then lend you the recorded material. Buy a couple of videotapes or DVRs for your recording requests. You can watch the taped program at the library or at a TV lab on campus.

Many channels provide a wonderful feature called *closed-captioning*, a written transcript of everything said during the broadcast that appears on the bottom of television screen. This feature was created specifically for individuals who have hearing problems. However, millions of viewers with normal hearing use closed-captioning to help them better understand the spoken language. Using this television feature, you are able to read and understand words that you either missed or misunderstood. Closed-captioning can eliminate the problem of following somebody who speaks very fast or with a difficult accent. Finally, closed-captioning may help you to learn to spell better: The words you hear are spelled on the screen! You will notice over time though that sometimes the closed captioning includes misspellings.

Think
Critically

Closed-captioning may not be so helpful if you overuse it. The constant presence of printed words on your television screen may create a psychological dependency. Instead of listening to the spoken words and attempting to comprehend as much as possible, your eyes will be looking for these little helpers on the screen. Therefore, a balanced combination is necessary: Closed-captioning could be turned on for some programs and turned off for others.

Keep a piece of paper or a notebook with a pen near your television set or a radio. Create a useful habit for yourself: Whenever you are watching television and hear an interesting expression, a new word, or a name, write it down. (If you do not write it down immediately after you heard it, you will probably forget it in several minutes!) After the program is over, or at a later time, get a dictionary and translate the words you have written down. Go over the list several times, and try to memorize the words and their translations. Students who follow this simple advice say that it allows them to add from three to five words daily to their active vocabulary! (Many words may later be forgotten, of course, because they are not used in conversations or written assignments; but still these words could remain in our memory and could be recalled.)

Different Conversational Styles

Turn on your television set and do some channel surfing: Go through all the channels you can receive. Listen to what people say on television. Many foreigners unfamiliar with the English language think everyone speaks English in the same way, but that is not true. Americans speak with different accents. There are different styles of language communication: official or formal, conversational, professional, and so on. If you want to be proficient in the language, you will have to learn more about the existing styles.

It will be difficult for you to compare different American accents while watching television because you do not have direct access to thousands of local stations across the country. Besides, even though there are noticeable accents in different areas like New York, Texas, Louisiana, Boston, Minnesota, and others, television announcers and news anchors rarely speak with a strong local accent.

What might be interesting is to observe different styles of conversation and communication. For example, observe the style used by television professionals who read the morning or evening news on the major networks: Their speech is usually fast, smooth, non-repetitive, and often filled with examples and colorful comparisons (see also *CNN Headline News* as an illustration). If a show is designed for children, notice how slowly everybody speaks (check, for instance, Nickelodeon in the early evening or the Cartoon Network). Do not be embarrassed to watch children's shows: The language is not filled with professional jargon, and the spoken sentences are usually very short. By contrast, look at the nightly discussions on MSNBC, especially when lawyers, professors, and politicians participate. The debates are spontaneous, people speak fast, and the language is often technical. If you would like to try a difficult task, check MTV or VH1. Most of the time, you will be watching music clips. Use closed-captioning (if available) when you try to follow the songs' lyrics: Even many native speakers have a hard time understanding the words! The songs may be viewed as modern poetry, a symbolic and often grotesque view of contemporary life.

A Homework Assignment

One of the most interesting ways to understand another culture is to listen to its music and songs. If you are not familiar with the contemporary western rock, rap, or pop music, take a small step forward. From MTV or VH1, select one video clip and tape it. Sometimes these stations provide closed-captioning that will make it easy for you to write down the song's lyrics: Play the tape several times, look at the screen, and copy the words. If there is no closed-captioning provided, just ask a native to help you understand and write down the words. After this, try to interpret the song: its content, a hidden context, and the expressed emotions. See what types of rhymes, allegories, and metaphors were used in this song. Remember, you don't have to like a song to analyze it.

TV is also known for its interesting reports and a variety of discussion-based reality shows. The style is primarily conversational and very close to the style many students use on campus. For comparison, watch movies made 40, 50, and even 60 years ago on American Movies Classics (AMC) or Turner Classic Movies (TCM). (Or compare old television shows from the 1960s to the 1980s, which are featured on the Nickelodeon and TVLand channels in the evening.) Notice the conversational style in those movies and older TV shows: The words are clearly articulated, and rules of grammar are carefully followed. Will you find it different from the language of the contemporary movies?

American Television Talk Shows

Talk shows appear in the mornings and afternoons and usually feature one or occasionally two or more hosts, who chat with each other and then chat with invited guests. Most of these shows have a live audience, usually a few hundred people. Such shows are typically pre-recorded and edited before being aired several hours later. If you take a look at a television guide, you will find that television networks offer (depending on the day and time of the year) from four to seven daily talk shows!

With all of the available high-tech television productions, action movies, and sensational news, how is it possible for talk shows to attract their audience and be profitable? In the age of the Internet and 24-hour news coverage, will talk shows disappear from television? On the contrary, most popular American talk shows not only have high ratings, but are often more popular than all other programs offered by a network later in the day. There are several explanations for this. First, the shows are personal: The language is simple—quite different from well-organized and grammatically correct language used by news anchors. Second, talk shows are hosted by popular individuals, whose appearance becomes an event by itself. Such names as David Letterman (late night), Jay Leno (late night), Oprah Winfrey, Barbara Walters, Ellen Degeneres, Dr. Phil, Bill O'Reilly, and Larry King are familiar to almost every American. Third, many of these shows feature popular national and international celebrities who use their appearance to promote a new movie, book, concert tour, or album. Some talk show hosts like Oprah and Dr. Phil discuss serious and dramatic issues designed to help viewers with problems. Others, like Jay Leno (NBC), David Letterman (CBS), Bill Maher (HBO), and Jimmy Kimmel (ABC) use a comedic format to entertain the guests and the viewers with flashy jokes and sharp comments. They appear after 11 PM.

Other shows do not include well-known guests but follow a different entertainment format, called sensationalism, selecting a bizarre or weird topic for its shock value and openly discussing it on the air. As a rule, people who are involved in these stories are invited to sit and talk in front of the audience. Hosts invite guests who might share their first sexual experiences or talk about how they hate their parents, how they love to drink blood, or run around naked. People with serious psychological problems or who have been abused by their parents, betrayed by friends, or failed in life are frequent guest of these shows. The participants may scream and shout at each other, use profanity, and throw objects.

Many international students wonder about people who become guests of these shows: How could one agree to share his or her intimate and embarrassing secrets in front of an audience of millions? There is no definitive answer to this question. Keep in mind, though, there are many individuals who dream about being on national television and would use almost anything to get their "15 minutes of fame." Also, some Americans are socialized by parents, other adults, and the media to be "themselves" and not to be ashamed of who they are and what is happening to them. For some, this personal sense of independence is part of their identity. Not every person, of course, accepts this psychology, but some do and feel absolutely fine telling everybody their deepest secrets.

Many Americans have a very low opinion of these types of talk shows and never watch them. So when you watch one of these shows, do not think that all Americans agree with their nature and content.

Television Dramas and Sitcoms

Television dramas and sitcoms together make up more than half of the programming featured by major networks. Such shows are weekly episodes staged and recorded in advance. (If the show is not new, it may appear daily as a *re-run*). Dramas usually feature plots of a serious nature, whereas a *sitcom* (meaning situation comedy) is meant to be funny. You will have your personal preferences and taste so it is impossible to give advice on what to watch.

For educational purposes, however, take a look at several of the most popular shows, which at different times have received top popularity ratings. Note how different these shows are. Compare, for example, *Seinfeld, Frazier,* and *Friends*, three urban sitcoms that are set in large cities like New York and Seattle. (These shows air only as re-runs now.) Then compare *30 Rock* and *Grey's Anatomy*, all featuring contemporary young American professionals. Cartoons are supposed to be for children, but you should examine *The Simpsons*, a cartoon show that features mature topics and sarcasm. To recall what you watch, use the following observation list for your comparisons.

TV Shows Observation List

✓ Describe the main character or characters, supporting characters, place or places where major events unfold. Write the network or channel name.

✓ Describe a personal profile of the major character or characters (age, occupation, major interests in life, and some psychological characteristics).

✓ Describe what kinds of problems main characters face and how they decide to solve them. Of course, they face different problems and use a variety of solutions; however, you are interested in finding a common pattern in their behavior. What is "American" in their behavior?

✓ For comparison purpose, try to find any similarities and differences between the main character of the show and some popular television or literary characters from your home country.

Politics on Television

In addition to the textbook and lectures, you can get a lot of information about American politics and public life by pushing the power button on your television remote control. Remember, American politics depicted on television is not a precise reflection of contemporary American life. You cannot make generalizations about the entire society simply by watching news and politics covered on television. But you may learn something about the country and its political and cultural traditions. Television stations and networks compete for viewers like you. They want you to watch *their* news and not the news broadcast by their competitors. One of the most successful ways they do this is by bringing you the news earlier than other companies do, or by providing you with more details about the events. Therefore, American coverage of local, national, and international events is based on a desire to bring the first so-called "breaking news" to your home. An old journalist joke goes, "If a dog bites a man it's not news. If a man bites a dog, that's news!" Not surprisingly, you may expect that a mayor's speech during a new park opening would not attract many viewers whereas a serious car accident would.

American television offers two versions of news: local and network news. Local news covers events close to your home. It features so-called eyewitness reports and interviews about regional events such as fires, injuries, local exhibitions, local weather, and sports. Occasionally, some experts are invited to do analyses of the stories, but it is less common than direct coverage of events from the location where events happen or from "beats," the locations where something is expected to occur. Watching local news can provide you with interesting stories and useful examples for class discussions and papers.

Network news is usually shorter than local news and designed to fit into a standard 30-minute format. The focus of prime-time network news is national and international conflicts, elections, natural disasters, political statements, negotiations, and other major developments. All networks provide evening analytical news programs, such as *20/20* (ABC), *Sixty Minutes* (CBS), or *Dateline* (NBC), and other programs dealing with issues of public concern. Usually, the reporters assigned to host the news or analytical news programs gain national recognition and become celebrities, such as Katie Couric (CBS), Brian Williams (NBC), and Charles Gibson (ABC).

Analysis of the News

If you are looking for detailed analyses of American public life and international developments, you have to watch special programs designed for these purposes. One of the oldest and most highly regarded political talk shows is *Meet the Press*. This one-hour program airs every Sunday morning on NBC. The format of the show consists of two or three interview segments with guests of national and international importance (public officials, political leaders, and journalists) followed by a discussion at the end of each segment. Like most political talk shows, *Meet the Press* features people of different political affiliations and ideologies. Host Tim Russert allows his guests to say as much as they want without confronting them. However, at the end of the show, he always expresses his point of view, which is usually critical. If you want to follow serious discussions and do not need to be entertained, you will definitely enjoy this show and may learn from it.

As we mentioned earlier, it is always fine to record the show that you are watching, especially when the topic or subject of the discussion is important to you. In many cases, you can obtain a free copy of a show transcript by downloading it from the show website. Go to the network home page and find a link to the show you are looking for. The transcripts are not posted for a long time: They usually only stay on a site from one to three weeks and then are replaced by more recent transcripts.

For your history classes, do not miss the History and Discovery channels. They air a great variety of documentaries and special programs featuring people who made history in the United States: presidents, politicians, generals, writers, and many other great individuals. Many of these programs are shown several times during the week, so look at the schedule and pick the best time.

A Homework Assignment

Choose one weekday and watch *Hannity and Colmes* (or a similar debate-style program). If you are busy at the time, ask somebody to record it if you do not have a recording device. You may also get a copy of the most recent transcripts from the show's web page. The show is designed in a special way. One of the hosts represents the liberal (on the left) position; the other host, actually sitting to the right of the other, represents the conservative position (on the right). Take a piece of paper and divide it in two halves with a vertical line. Practice your note-taking skills by writing down and comparing the arguments of both sides: Use the left half of the page for the liberal arguments and the right half for the conservative ones. Which arguments sound more compelling to you? Which arguments do you like or dislike: on the "left" or on the "right"? Is there a major difference between these two types of arguments? If yes, what did you notice?

Sports on Television and Your Education

You can watch sporting events on all major networks. In addition, local stations may broadcast the most important games of favorite local teams. The most prominent sports channel is ESPN. Companies such as Versus, TNT, and USA also show many sporting events. Sporting events are broadcast for pure entertainment purpose. Some might ask, How can one study anything from watching baseball or football?

There are several ways to learn from watching American sports. First, knowledge about sports helps you better understand American culture, its history, and heritage. Currently, the most popular American sports are baseball, basketball, football (often called "American football" in other countries), ice hockey, and golf. There are many manuals available in bookstores that tell you about how these sports were developed and what their rules are.

But surely the best source of knowledge about any of these sports might be a friend who grew up in America. Watch a couple of games with him or her, and try to understand what you are watching. You do not have to become a sports fan, but watching sports can enrich your vocabulary. Many words and expressions used in the game are part of American conversational vocabulary. Some people use these words more often than others, but most Americans can understand them. For example, the word *homerun* is from baseball where the exact meaning is to hit the ball over the fence and score a run. In conversations and printed stories, this word is often used to indicate a true success or a decisive victory, breakthrough, or defeat. Write and remember some phrases and words you hear on sports channels. Ask for their interpretation. Try to use some of these words in your daily conversations. You will see how many people around you will appreciate it.

One cannot see everything about a room by looking at a mirror's reflection of it. Indeed, the media can give you only a reflection of American life. Remember that the American media, above all, is private business. The networks, newspapers, and local and cable stations constantly compete for the viewer's attention. You may have different opinions about the media, but they should not prevent you from examining all types and learning from them. They are great sources for developing your language skills. You can expand your vocabulary by reading a newspaper daily. You could learn the nuances of American life examining television talk shows, dramas, and sitcoms. You will learn to better navigate the maze of American public life by listening to radio talk shows. Music and sports are fun to watch but they can also be used for educational purposes. Become an active viewer, listener, and reader. The rule is simple. Always ask yourself: "What can I learn from this?"

A Homework Assignment

Ask somebody who is familiar with baseball, football, and basketball to explain to you the meanings of the following expressions: *Three strikes and you're out, seventh inning stretch, the bases are loaded, a wild pitch, a home run, fourth down and inches, a three-point shot, a two-minute warning.* Write the explanations. Compose your own sentences (not related to sport) that would contain these expressions. Share what you have written with your professor or a friend who is fluent in English. Ask her to interpret these sentences. Compare their interpretations with yours.

The Internet

Access to high-speed Internet has become affordable in most areas of the United States, and the Internet has exploded as a source of media. There are chat rooms, blogs, and video databases such as YouTube and myspace.com® that have developed and host a tremendous subscriber base. These reality forums give the average individual access to a public space to develop a media persona. The Internet is full of great varieties of multimedia, like videos, music, text, and photography. Music files called MP3s can be downloaded and saved on small players that have enormous storage capacity.

At colleges and universities, the Internet has been integrated into many courses, and professors use virtual classrooms like WebCT and Blackboard to support their instruction and sometimes to deliver the entire course. It is likely that when you view the course offerings at your school, you will have the option to choose from a variety of modes of delivery of courses. Distance learning courses are ones where you never meet your professor or the other students in the class; hybrid courses meet one or two days in a classroom, and one day online; traditional courses have heavy online support.

Make sure that you meet with an academic advisor and your International Student Advisor before selecting any of these alternative course delivery models. Federal law restricts F and J visa students to only three credits of online study per semester to make up their full-time load.

Conclusion

As writer John Updike once said in one of his novels, "Black is a shade of brown. So is white if you look." Indeed, sometimes similarities and differences are not as dramatic as we believed they were. Things previously unfamiliar become recognizable. Difficult problems are solved and knots are untied.

John Foster Dulles—a famous American diplomat—once said that the measure of success is not whether you have a tough problem to deal with, but whether it's the same problem you had last year. We hope that this book will help you develop new skills so you can handle today's difficulties with confidence and clarity.

We hope that this book has helped you to understand the United States a little better. Before you close it and go, we wish to give our last piece of advice: Please live with your eyes wide open and never lose your optimism. Follow the good examples of others. Your experience in the United States will change you and should make your life better. You then can make the world better in your own way.

Your success depends on you.

Appendix

A Sample List of Evaluation Services

World Education Services, Inc.
P.O. Box 745
Old Chelsea Station
New York, NY 10113-0745
Phone: (212) 966-6311
Fax: (212) 966-6395
Email: *info@wes.org*
Website: *www.wes.com*

World Educational Credentials Evaluators
P.O. Box 726
Herndon, VA 22070
Phone: (703) 689-0894
Fax: (703) 707-0291
Email: *wecewellington@erols.com*
Website: *http://users.erols.com/wecewellington*

Educational Credential
    Evaluators, Inc.
P.O. Box 92970
Milwaukee, WI 53202-0970
Phone: (414) 289-3400
Fax: (414) 289-3411
Email: *eval@ece.org*
Website: *www.ece.org*

International Consultants of Delaware,
    Inc.
109 Barksdale Professional Center
Newark, Delaware 19711
Phone: (302) 737-8715
Fax: (302) 737-8756
Email: *icd@icdel.com*

International Education Research Foundation, Inc.
P.O. Box 3665
Culver City, CA 90231-3665
Phone: (310) 285-9451
Fax: (310) 342-7086
Email: *info@ierf.org*
Website: *www.ierf.org*

College Guides

Fiske Guide to Colleges 2008, E. Fiske. Naperville, IL: Sourcebooks, Inc.

The Best 361 Colleges, 2007 edition. Princeton Review. New York: Random House.

The Insider's Guide to the Colleges, 2008: 34th edition. Yale Daily News staff. New York: St. Martin's.

U.S. News Ultimate College Guide 2007, Inc. U.S. News & World Report. Naperville, IL: Sourcebooks, Inc.

References

America the Beautiful. Greenwich, CT: Brompton Books, 1988.

The Associated Press. Circulation at the Top 20 Newspapers. Press release, April 30, 2007.

Brislin, R, and P. Pedersen. *Cross-Cultural Orientation Programs.* New York: Gardner Press, 1976.

Campbell, J. *The Year that Defined American Journalism.* London: Routledge, 2006.

Cherry, Conrad, Betty A. DeBerg, and Amanda Porterfield. *Religion on Campus.* Chapel Hill: University of North Carolina Press, 2001.

Ellis, A. *Reason and Emotion in Psychotherapy.* New York: Lyle Stuart, 1962.

Erskine, H. "The Polls: Women's Role." *Public Opinion Quarterly* 35 (1971): 275–90.

Fast, Julius. *Body Language.* New York: Pocket Books, 1988.

Federal Bureau of Investigation. *Crime in the United States, 1995.* Washington, DC: U.S. Government Printing Office, 1996.

Gallup, G. *The Gallup Poll: Public Opinion 1984.* Princeton, NJ: Gallup, 1985.

Gordon, L., and S. Shaffer. *Mom, Can I Move Back in with You?* New York: Penguin/Tarcher, 2004.

Gould, S. J. "This View of Life: Unusual Unity." *Natural History* 106 (1997): 20–23.

Graber, D. *Mass Media and American Politics.* Washington DC: CQ Press, 2006.

Greenberg Research. Press release, December 5, 2006.

Gudykunst, William, and Michael Bond. "Intergroup Relations across Cultures," in *Handbook of Cross-Cultural Psychology,* edited by John Berry et al., pp. 119–61. Boston: Allyn and Bacon, 1997.

Hill, J. "Affirmative Action: Roots to Success." *Los Angeles Times,* March 13, 1997.

Institute for International Education. *Open Doors Report 2007.* New York: Institute for International Education, 2007.

Institute for Social Research, the University of Michigan. *General Social Surveys, 1972–2004.* Ann Arbor: The University of Michigan.

Jamison, K. *Touched with Fire: Manic-Depressive Illness and the Artistic Temperament.* New York: Free Press, 1993.

Keister, L. *Getting Rich: A Study of Wealth Mobility in America.* New York: Cambridge University Press, 2005.

Kennedy, J. F. Foreword. In *Challenge to Americans: The Struggle We Face and How to Help Win It.* New York: The Advertising Council, 1963.

Levy, D. *Tools of Critical Thinking.* Boston: Allyn & Bacon, 1997.

Lewis, M. *Multicultural Health Psychology.* Boston: Allyn & Bacon, 2001.

Macionis, J. *Sociology.* Upper Saddle River, NJ: Prentice Hall, 2005.

Maley, A. "Crossing the Cultural Rubicon." *Practical English Teaching* 13 (June 1993): 1–3.

Norrander, B. "The Evolution of the Gender Gap." *Public Opinion Quarterly* Winter 63 (1999): 566–67.

Our American Government. Washington, DC: U.S. Government Printing Office, 1993.

Palmer, Barbara, and Dennis Simon. *Breaking the Political Glass Ceiling: Women and Congressional Election.* London: Routledge, 2006.

Perls, Fritz. *The Gestalt Approach and Eyewitness to Therapy.* Palo Alto: CA: Science and Behavior Books, 1973.

Phillips, D. "Is a Culture a Factor in Air Crashes?" *The Washington Post,* March, 18, 1998: A17.

Shiraev, E. and D. Levy. *Cross-Cultural Psychology, 3rd ed.* Boston: Allyn & Bacon, 2007.

Shiraev, E., and R. Sobel. *People and Their Opinions.* New York: Longman, 2006.

Stern, H. H. *Issues and Opinions in Language Teaching.* New York: Oxford University Press, 1992.

Stossel, John. *Myths, Lies, and Downright Stupidity.* New York: Hyperion, 2006.

Strong, B., C. DeVault, and B. Sayad. *The Marriage and Family Experience.* Belmont, CA: ITP, 1998.

Tsytsarev, S. "Pathological Anger in 'Crimes of Passion,'" *Security Journal,* 9 (1997): 203–4.

Tsytsarev, S., and G. Grodnitsky. "Anger and Criminality," in *Anger Disorders,* edited by H. Kassinove, pp. 91–108. Washington, DC: Taylor & Francis, 1995.